# healing drinks

# healing drinks

## anne mcintyre

Gaia Books Limited

**A GAIA ORIGINAL**

Books from Gaia celebrate the vision of Gaia, the self-sustaining living Earth, and seek to help its readers live in greater personal and planetary harmony.

Editorial Mary Pickles, Pip Morgan
Designer Sara Mathews
Photographer Adrian Swift
Managing Editor Pip Morgan
Production Lyn Kirby
Direction Joss Pearson, Patrick Nugent

**Disclaimer**
The recipes and suggestions in this book are to be used at the reader's sole discretion and risk. Always consult a doctor if you are in doubt about a medical condition.

First published in the United Kingdom in 2000 by
Gaia Books Ltd, 66 Charlotte Street, London W1P 1LR
and 20 High Street, Stroud, Gloucestershire GL5 1AZ

ISBN 1 85675 180 5

A catalogue record of this book is available from the British Library.

Printed and bound by Dai Nippon Printing Co, Hong Kong

10 9 8 7 6 5 4 3

# contents

# foreword

Reading this book will revolutionize the way you think about vegetables, fruit and all things herbal.

Like many other health-conscious people, I'd thrown fruit and vegetables in a blender and downed the (sometimes less than delicious) result with the grim determination of someone who knew they were doing themself good.

No doubt I was, because all the experts on health and nutrition now agree that eating at least five portions of fruit and vegetables a day should substantially reduce your risk of heart disease and cancer. But though – as someone with a university degree in food science and nutrition – I knew the benefits, as a human being I was missing something.

In a nutshell, I didn't have the benefit of author Anne McIntyre's vast experience as a medical herbalist, combined with her knowledge of plants and herbs, gained through collecting food and plant medicines from the wild.

Anne doesn't approach the subject of health drinks in a haphazard suck-it-and-see sort of way. She describes in a clear, logical manner the benefits of liquids, and the techniques and equipment you'll need to get started making everything from juices and soups to wines and liqueurs.

She focuses on 25 of the top healthy ingredients to use in drinks, and then gives over several chapters to the delicious, yet simple-to-make recipes. Here we find out what we all really want to know – how to make drinks that make us more beautiful, may help to protect us against disease and even lift our mood. For sceptics, the scientific reasoning behind each formula is explained.

What will impress you most about this book is just how tasty the recipes are, and how much you will want to try them all. A personal favourite is Malaysian Ginger and Lemon Tea (see p. 63) – I don't know if I like it best because it reminds me of holidays in the Far East, or because it really does seem to give me a boost when my defences are low.

Whatever your taste preference or health needs, I'm certain this book will supply you with several health-giving drinks that will quickly become firm favourites.

*Happy experimenting and good health!*

**Angela Dowden**

**Angela Dowden** is one of Britain's
leading health and nutrition journalists.
A Fellow of The Royal Society of Health
and a Member of the Guild of Health
Writers, Angela regularly contributes to
national newspapers, such as the *Daily
Mail*, and to magazines, such as *Zest*,
*Woman*, *Healthy* and *Top Santé*.

Angela is author of *Are You Getting
Enough Vitamins and Minerals?* (1999),
co-author of *The Consumer Guide to
Vitamins* (1996), contributor to *Healthy
Options* (1997) and consultant nutrition
editor on *Eat Better, Feel Better* (1998).

healing drinks

# introduction

# introduction

Liquid is vital to life, whether it is drunk in the form of plain, unadulterated water or in exotic concoctions on festive occasions, and drinks fulfil a whole range of functions in our lives. Certainly they may satisfy our immediate needs by quenching our thirst, but they can also cool and refresh us on a hot day or warm us on a cold winter's day. Drinks can be packed with nutrients that nourish and strengthen us, providing the raw materials and energy to heal us in mind and body when we are unwell. They have the ability to increase our vitality and even our longevity, as well as to console and calm us in times of stress or trauma.

For centuries drinking has formed part of both social and religious ceremonies all over the world, and it still plays a symbolic role in our lives today. On social and business occasions we often drink together almost as a ritual to ease communication. With a drink we toast the health of a friend, the happiness of a bridal couple and the birth of a new baby, or celebrate a wedding anniversary, a birthday or Christmas. Or we may simply enjoy a good chat over a drink.

## The importance of water

When we consider that the body is made up of 75 per cent water, it is hardly surprising that we need to drink regularly to keep our bodies functioning well. Adults lose around 2.25-3.5 litres (4-6 pints) of water every day (more if we take a lot of physical exercise): 0.6 litre (1 pint) in perspiration, 1.2 litres (2 pints) in breathing out and 1.8 litres (3 pints) of urine. This liquid must all be replaced. In fact our bodies can survive longer without food than they can without water. The right balance of water is essential for the function of every cell in the body.

Sufficient water taken in one form or another is necessary to bulk out waste products in the bowel to prevent constipation and subsequent bowel problems. It is also needed to flush wastes and toxins out through the skin in the form of sweat and via the bladder as urine to prevent irritation to the kidneys or bladder. During a fever, diarrhoea or vomiting, it is vital to drink plenty of liquid to prevent dehydration. After a night on the town, drinking copious amounts of water or fruit juice will flush out the kidneys and reduce the likelihood of a hangover.

Many of us tend not to drink as much as we need to keep ourselves in tiptop condition. If plain water does not seem inviting enough, there are numerous more flavoursome ways to take water into the body. The recipes in this book – for fruit juices, smoothies, vegetable juices, cocktails of vegetables or fruits, soups and teas – will entice even reluctant drinkers to imbibe a little more.

## Tea

Whether it is Chinese, Indian or herbal, tea is a perfectly natural drink containing no artificial additives, and has been part of our lives for thousands of years. Apart from water, many of us drink more tea than any other drink and we can make good use of this medium by finding a repertoire of health-promoting teas that appeal to our taste buds. Each herbal tea has not only its own unique flavour but also a range of medicinal benefits well known to those in the world of herbal medicine. The herbal teas in this book have been chosen for their therapeutic effects as well as their light aromatic flavours, and make a delightful change from the normal cuppa.

Because "normal" tea contains caffeine it has had a bad press during the last few years, particularly since stress plays a significant part in the development of health problems and caffeine exacerbates the effects of stress. More recently, however, tea (Chinese, Indian or Japanese) has been found to contain anti-oxidants in the form of flavonoids. These help to protect the body against free radicals, which contribute to chronic illness such as heart disease and cancer. One of the flavonoids, catechin, is also found in apple and grape skins. One drawback concerning tea consumption is that it contains polyphenols, which can interfere with iron absorption. For this reason, it is best to drink tea between meals rather than with your food, particularly if you are vegetarian.

## Coffee

In Europe, the Middle East, and North, Central and South America, coffee is the preferred stimulant for regular intake. Many people agree that it is hard to find a more attractive bevvy to get them up in the morning and keep them going throughout a busy day, but those who drink a lot of coffee may have a price to pay. Caffeine may over-stimulate the nervous system and exacerbate the effects of stress. It can lead to tiredness, irritability, anxiety or insomnia, and is a common cause of headaches, migraine, hormone imbalances and indigestion. Decaffeinated coffee can reduce the harmful impact on the nervous system in determined coffee drinkers. Alternatively, adding cardamom, as they do in the Middle East, helps to neutralize the effects of caffeine. Strong coffee made in a cafetière or percolator has been shown to raise blood cholesterol, increasing the risk of arterial and heart disease. However, both ordinary and decaffeinated coffee contain antioxidants which actually help to reduce the risk of heart disease. The laxative and diuretic effects of coffee can be useful, but may have you needing the bathroom when it is not convenient.

## Juices

Raw fruit and vegetable juices are said to be the richest available sources of vitamins, minerals and enzymes. Drunk in this form, these pass rapidly into the blood stream because they require very little breaking down in the digestive tract. Juices seem to radiate pure life force. People who drink fresh juices regularly say that since they have been doing so they have felt more energetic, their skin has been clearer, their hair shinier and their resilience to infection greater. Specific fruit and vegetable juices, chosen for their therapeutic properties, can be used to treat minor health disorders such as skin problems, sluggish bowels, arthritis and a whole range of other problems that are discussed in the following pages. Use freshly squeezed or extracted juices for the recipes whenever possible and drink them immediately to derive maximum benefit. All that you need to make your own juices is a good juicer (see Appendix for more details).

## Milk drinks

Smoothies, delicious, thick, creamy blends of fruits, fruit juices and milk or yogurt, have been popular for a while on the west coast of North America and in hot countries all over the world. They are now fast catching on as fashionable drinks in Britain and Europe. Certainly, there is every reason for smoothies to be popular. As well as tasting absolutely delicious, they are filling and nutritious. In fact, they make an ideal breakfast or a snack for any busy person who does not have time to prepare a proper meal since they are quick and easy to make – all you need are the ingredients and a blender. Because smoothies are cold, however, they are not the best form of liquid intake in the winter or for ayone who suffers from poor circulation and a sluggish metabolism. (Warm milk drinks with plenty of spices are preferable in these instances.)

All the milky drinks in this book can be prepared using cow's, goat's or ewe's milk products. Alternatively if you are vegan or suffer from a lactose intolerance, you can use soya milk, rice milk, almond milk or oat milk, all of which are suitable for people who have a tendency to allergies, frequent respiratory infections, catarrh, menopausal symptoms or bowel problems. If you are watching your weight or are concerned about a tendency to raised cholesterol, high blood pressure or heart disease, choose low-fat milk and yogurt. Fat is necessary for the absorption of vitamins A and D and calcium (which are fat soluble) so it is important not to cut it out of your diet entirely. For this reason it is best to use full-fat milk for growing children and those concerned about osteoporosis including menopausal women and the elderly.

## Soups

Soups come in all shapes and forms from a light, thin starter for a meal to a thick, textured soup, with chunky vegetables and grains or pulses, that makes a meal in itself. Eaten hot in winter, their wonderful warming properties are enhanced by plenty of onions, garlic, leeks and pungent spices. In summer cucumber, lettuce and avocado soups are refreshing eaten cool or chilled with light aromatic herbs such as mint and coriander leaves. Soups are always tastier and more nutritious when made with real vegetable or chicken stock.

## Ingredients

When buying the raw ingredients for your drinks, it is important to buy the best quality you can. The fresher the produce, the richer it is in valuable nutrients. Certain nutrients, for example vitamins A and C and folic acid, diminish during storage so buy small quantities of fruit and vegetables at a time and use them quickly. If you want to make drinks with ingredients that are out of season it is possible to use frozen, tinned or dried versions, though the results in some cases may be inferior in taste, nutrition and vitality. If you are using tinned fruit choose fruit that is preserved in fruit juice or water rather than a heavy syrup. When using dried fruit try to find fruit that has been sun-dried rather than sulphur-dried, even though it may not look quite so attractive; sulphur can cause allergic reactions in some people.

Buy organic fruit and vegetables whenever possible to avoid the risk of health problems related to pesticides. You will not have to remove the peel from most organic produce. It is worth noting that many vital nutrients lie just below the skin, as in the case of potatoes and apples. Always choose ripe fruit as they will give a sweeter taste and smoother texture to your juices and smoothies.

Alcohol-free drinks are a fashionable way to get you looking and feeling your best. The recipes in this book are not just boring alternatives for teetotallers or health fanatics, but have been selected to stimulate the senses and scintillate the taste buds, at the same time as improving health and vitality. Enlivened with a variety of herbs and spices, these drinks are bursting with ingredients to keep us feeling on top of the world, but they will also enhance the healing process when we are not at our best. Vitamins, minerals and trace elements, protein, essential fatty acids, complex carbohydrates and a whole range of therapeutic phytochemicals are all here, playing leading roles in delicious drinks with which we can truly toast your good health. Cheers!

1

key ingredients

# key ingredients

Apples, pears, lemons and apricots, carrot, beetroot, cabbage, cucumber and spinach, barley, oats, yogurt and almonds are among the foodstuffs which provide the basis for the majority of the drinks in this book. They are chosen for a variety of good reasons. They are all familiar to us and are not hard to find – in fact, they will already feature widely in the kitchens and gardens of most readers. Combined together and brought to life by the addition of aromatic herbs and spices, they taste not good but delicious. Just because the drinks in this book are here to enhance your health, they do not necessarily have to taste like medicines.

Carbohydrates, our main source of energy, are found in fruits and starchy foods like oats, barley and carrots. Soluble fibre in such grains, fruits and vegetables slows down the rate of digestion in the stomach and intestine, so providing a steady flow of energy as the food is digested and absorbed. It helps to maintain a stable sugar level in the blood and has been shown to reduce harmful cholesterol levels, thus it is believed to reduce the risk of arterial and heart disease.

Vitamins and minerals are vital to every function in the body and can be obtained only from what we eat and drink. The complexities of the interactions between vitamins and minerals, as well as other vital constituents of food, are achieved in nature through a nutrient-rich diet. The same result cannot be achieved by the daily consumption of artificial and isolated supplements. Many of the fruits and vegetables in this chapter contain antioxidants, substances with the ability to prevent oxidation in the body, which causes the release of harmful free radicals. (Free radicals contribute to heart disease, cancer, degenerative disease, lowered immunity and the aging process.) The antioxidants vitamins A, C and E, selenium and many carotenes and flavonoids have been shown to exert their beneficial influence far better when derived from food sources than when taken in the form of supplements.

Herbs and spices included in this chapter have been chosen for their versatility and for their delightful ability to enhance the flavour of the ingredients they accompany in these drinks recipes. As if this were not enough, basil, coriander, cinnamon, ginger, garlic, ginseng, lemon balm, thyme and rosemary are some of the world's greatest healers. Abundant in therapeutic constituents, such as volatile oils, tannins, bitters, saponins, mucilage and flavonoids, they also offer a wealth of medicinal benefits which have been praised by shaman, physician, apothecary and herbalist alike since time immemorial.

# carrot *Daucus carota*

The humble carrot is a storehouse of nutrients, antioxidant vitamins A, B and C, and valuable minerals including iron, calcium and potassium. Eaten regularly carrots are a wonderful restorative remedy, particularly for those feeling weak and debilitated, or when recovering from illness or stress. In children and adolescents they promote growth and vitality, and help to build healthy tissue and skin. Their iron content increases haemoglobin levels and helps combat anaemia, and their beta-carotene is excellent for promoting good night vision and for general care of the eyes. Recent research has indicated that beta-carotene may inhibit the development of tumours, particularly in smoking-related cancer in the lungs and pancreas.

Carrots were first cultivated in Afghanistan and the Near East and were well known to our ancestors. They were used by the ancient Greeks, notably by Hippocrates in 430BC as a tonic for the stomach, and later by Galen as a remedy for flatulence. Carrot seeds were used in Crete in Roman times in their then famous "mithridate" which protected the body against the effects of all sorts of poisons. In the 1960s Russian scientists extracted and isolated an ingredient, called Daucarine, which was shown to dilate blood vessels, particularly those in the head, and to protect against arterial and heart disease. Fresh carrot juice with honey and a little water, taken daily by the tablespoon, is recommended in Russia to cure colds and coughs.

Renowned for their digestive properties, carrots deservedly used to be referred to as "great friends of the intestine". In soups and juices, carrots will help to regulate intestinal activity and promote normal bowel function, so they help remedy both constipation and diarrhoea. They soothe the mucous membranes throughout the digestive tract, reducing irritation and inflammation. Plain carrot soup can be given even to small infants to treat acute diarrhoea and digestive problems. A carrot juice fast is a well-known cleansing therapy for the liver (for more information on juice fasting, see p. 149), and carrots used to be a popular remedy in France for liver and gall-bladder problems. A glass of carrot juice taken half an hour before breakfast can expel worms and is an excellent remedy for threadworms in children.

## Healing qualities

• Carrot stimulates the appetite and enhances the secretion of digestive juices. It makes a good remedy for flatulence, colic, colitis, irritable bowel syndrome, intestinal infections and peptic ulcers.

• Carrot's diuretic effect helps relieve fluid retention and cystitis. Its detoxifying effect is useful in treating eczema and acne, and can help arthritis and gout.

• Expectorant properties help to liquify and expel mucus from the chest in coughs, bronchitis and asthma.

• Antiseptic properties help to prevent and treat bacterial and viral infections including respiratory infections and childhood diseases such as measles and chicken pox.

• Antioxidants enhance the efforts of the immune system and help to prevent damage caused by free radicals and protect against degenerative disease, particularly in the heart and circulation.

• Eating 1 or 2 carrots daily can lower blood cholesterol by over ten per cent and help to prevent heart and arterial disease.

*Cross references*
moroccan carrot soup, p. 53
cabbage and carrot juice, p. 75
carrot and rosemary juice, p. 83
hungarian beetroot and carrot
  cleanser, p. 100
danish carrot and dill soup, p. 107

# onion *Allium cepa*

The onion is often called "the king of vegetables" because of its pungent taste, culinary versatility and powerful antiseptic properties. Rich in vitamins A, B and C, it is a potent source of calcium, phosphorus, magnesium and iron. When raw, onion is a good digestive stimulant and liver tonic; when cooked, it can help relieve flatulence and chronic constipation. A tea of boiled onion skins can alleviate the unpleasant symptoms of diarrhoea.

A close relation of garlic, onion was venerated by the ancient Egyptians as a symbol of vitality and as a cure-all for many illnesses. Ancient records reveal its use in religious rites and healing as early as 4000BC. Its antiseptic qualities have proved effective against infectious diseases such as typhoid, cholera and the plague. As recently as World War II, vapours from onion paste reduced the pain and accelerated the healing of soldiers' wounds.

Healing drinks containing onions take a wide variety of forms – infusion, soup, wine, decoction, syrup and juice. You can use any variety of globe onion but not pickling onions. If you like your onions strong and pungent, try the smaller varieties – they are the ones that make your eyes water when you cut them open. Spanish and Italian red onions are milder than most and often sweet. The white and yellow varieties lose some of their strength when heated and infuse other foods with a sweet flavour.

Always check when buying globe onions that they feel firm to the touch and have a regular shape. If their red-brown or pale-coloured, papery skins look at all shrivelled, or if they feel soft at the top, they are likely to be bad. Onions with green sprouts at the top are probably past their best.

## Healing qualities

• Raw onion is powerfully antiseptic – it fights infectious bacteria, including *E. coli* and salmonella, and is effective against tuberculosis and infections of the urinary tract, such as cystitis.

• Onion's pungency increases blood circulation and causes sweating, useful in cold damp weather to ward off infection, bring down fevers, and sweat out colds and flu.

• Onion juice is excellent for sore throats, pharyngitis, rhinitis, colds, catarrh and sinusitis, breaking up mucous congestion.

• Onion's diuretic and blood-cleansing properties can counter fluid retention, urinary gravel, arthritis and gout.

• Onion's detoxifying effects relieve tiredness and exhaustion.

• Eating half a medium raw onion daily can significantly lower low-density lipoprotein cholesterol and help to prevent heart attacks. Both raw and cooked, onions lower blood pressure, thin the blood, dissolve blood clots and clear the blood of unhealthy fats.

*Cross references*
onion wine, p. 81
french onion soup, p. 97

# lemon *Citrus limon*

The tangy, refreshing lemon gives added zest to almost any drink, while imparting cleansing and immune-enhancing properties to your healthy cocktail of ingredients. It is a good source of vitamin C, vital for warding off infections and for speeding healing. Lemons also contain vitamins A and B and bioflavonoids, all precious antioxidants that help to slow the aging process, and limonene, a substance thought to block the action of cancer-causing chemicals. Pectin in the pulp of lemons lowers cholesterol, and so helps protect the arteries against disease.

Originally from northern India, the lemon was revered by the Romans who considered it an antidote to all poisons, even snakebites, in recognition of its excellent detoxifying effect in the body. The lemon is even depicted in one of the famous mosaics at Pompeii. To prevent sailors suffering from the skin disease scurvy, from 1700 onwards every English ship sailing for foreign parts was required by law to carry a supply of lemon or lime juice. British sailors subsequently became known as "Limeys".

Drunk in hot water each morning, one hour before eating, fresh lemon juice makes an excellent cleansing start to the day. It stimulates bile flow from the liver, the great detoxifying organ of the body, helping to aid digestion of fats. With olive oil, lemon juice will help dissolve gall-stones. Lemon juice is also a traditional remedy for a hangover. In a cup of hot water with honey and three cloves, it acts as a decongestant for colds, catarrh and sinusitis, and as a soothing expectorant for coughs. A little lemon juice in cold water makes a refreshing drink to allay thirst on a hot summer's day, or to cool a fever or help shake off infection.

Limes can be used interchangeably with lemons and you may find their taste is not as sour.

*"Lemons which have been used in the flavouring of cabbage leaves and other such insipids may be hung on old or unused garments and will help to preserve them by keeping away moths and other predators."*
Leonardo da Vinci, 16th-century Italian artist

## Healing qualities

• An excellent antiseptic to help ward off colds, coughs, sore throats and flu.

• Has a cooling effect in fevers as it stimulates sweating and a decongestant action in the respiratory system.

• Helps to neutralize excess acid in the stomach and protects the lining of the digestive tract, relieving digestive problems including hiccoughs, heartburn, nausea, constipation, haemorrhoids and worms.

• Its diuretic action speeds elimination of fluid and toxins via the kidneys and bladder. Good for fluid retention and arthritis.

• Lemon juice also acts as a urinary antiseptic, excellent for treating bladder and kidney infections.

• Has an antiseptic effect in the gut, helping to ward off stomach and bowel infections, including travellers' diarrhoea. Aids the elimination of wastes.

*Cross references*
malaysian ginger and lemon tea, p. 63
spiced lemonade, p. 77
elizabethan rosemary and
   lemon syrup, p. 89

# lemon balm

*Melissa officinalis*

*"Balm is sovereign for the brain, strengthening memory and powerfully chasing away melancholy."*
John Evelyn, 17th-century English diarist

The sweet, lemon-flavoured leaves of lemon balm make an excellent addition to fruit cups, wines and juices, while a cool infusion provides a refreshing drink for lazy summer days. Lemon balm is a wonderful remedy for the nerves, calming tension and anxiety, lifting low spirits and restoring energy when tired and run down. Its relaxing effects make lemon balm a good remedy for headaches and migraines. Taken regularly it is also excellent for stress-related digestive disorders such as poor appetite, nausea, colic, colitis, IBS and gastritis, and a mild infusion will calm nervous tummy upsets in children.

For more than 2,000 years lemon balm has been a favoured ingredient of many an elixir of life, particularly popular with the 11th-century Arab physician, Avicenna. For centuries it has been popular as a remedy for melancholia, lethargy, to strengthen memory and to restore youthful "vitality". Medieval monks incorporated lemon balm into "cordials" designed to "comfort the heart", to strengthen the heart and lift the spirits. Carmelite water – a well-known 17th-century preparation made by the Carmelite nuns as a restorative and to relieve nervous headaches and neuralgia – combined lemon balm with lemon peel, nutmeg and angelica root.

The green-leaved, gold and variegated varieties can be used interchangeably. Hot lemon balm tea is the perfect drink for anyone studying for exams. In fact, lemon balm used to be called "the scholars herb". It stimulates mental energy, improves concentration and memory, and at the same time calms the nerves. Taken hot, as in limeflower and lemon balm tea, it will bring down fevers by inducing sweating. A few leaves can be floated in drinks, such as Borage and Lemon Balm Fruit Cup, to help heal a broken heart, or added as a flavoursome garnish.

## Healing qualities

• Hot lemon balm drinks relieve fever, catarrhal congestion and sinusitis.

• Lemon balm's antiviral action is effective against flu, herpes simplex and mumps.

• Its antibacterial and antihistamine action makes lemon balm an excellent remedy for infections and allergies, including hay fever, eczema and inflammatory eye conditions.

• Reduces anxiety and depression through its influence on the part of the brain concerned with mood and temperament.

• Makes a relaxing nighttime drink for poor sleepers or to calm children at bedtime.

• Through its affinity to the heart lemon balm calms nervous palpitations and can help to reduce high blood pressure.

• In the reproduction tract lemon balm releases spasm and relieves menstrual pain. Lemon balm tea taken in the last few weeks of pregnancy can ease childbirth.

*Cross references*
french limeflower and lemon balm tea,
   p. 86
provence lavender and lemon balm
   tisane, p. 130
borage and lemon balm fruit cup, p. 143
lemon balm tea, p. 146

# coriander

*Coriander sativum*

The unique flavour of coriander leaf is delightful to many but not to everyone – the ancient Greeks named coriander after a bedbug (*koris*) because they considered its taste and smell unpleasant. Fresh coriander leaves are highly popular in Thai, Moroccan, Mexican, Chinese, Indonesian, African and South American cuisines, where their cooling effect creates an excellent balance to hot spicy food. In Ayurvedic medicine coriander leaves and seeds are used to remedy excess *pitta* (fire) and to relieve problems associated with excess heat, such as hot inflammatory joint conditions, digestive and urinary problems, conjunctivitis and skin rashes. The fresh leaves are rich in antioxidant vitamins A and C as well as niacin, calcium and iron, acting to enhance immunity, protect against degenerative disease and slow the aging process.

A native of Southern Europe and Western Asia, coriander was one of the first herbs to be used in cooking and as a medicine. It is mentioned in Sanskrit texts dating back almost 7,000 years, and the seeds have been found in Egyptian tombs dating back 3,000 years, including the tomb of Tutankhamun. In China during the Han dynasty (207BC-AD220) coriander seeds had a reputation as an aphrodisiac. The Romans introduced coriander into Western Europe and England where, at weddings in medieval times, the seeds were prepared in a drink that was drunk for its energizing and aphrodisiac properties and also as a digestive.

Fresh coriander leaves are delicious chopped into soups and vegetable juices, and blend particularly well with tomatoes, cucumber, avocado and lettuce. Their digestive properties are excellent to prevent and remedy wind and indigestion. Coriander seeds and leaves help to combat drowsiness after eating a large meal and, in soups and hot decoctions, boost energy and vitality and help to lessen the intoxicating effects of alcohol. Drinking coriander leaf juice or tea will help soothe hot itchy rashes as well as other allergies such as hay fever.

*"Mark that the juice of coriander blown up the nostrils restrains nosebleeds....And coriander is effective in tremors of the heart when its powder is given with borage water."*
The Herbarius Litnus, German manuscript, 1484

## Healing qualities

• The volatile oils in the seeds are antibacterial and help combat infection, particularly in the digestive tract. They make a good remedy for diarrhoea and gastroenteritis.

• Taken in hot teas, the seeds can be used to promote sweating to break a fever and to bring out the rash in eruptive infections such as measles and chicken pox.

• By stimulating immunity and acting as a decongestant, coriander (particularly the seeds, taken in hot teas) helps remedy colds, flu, coughs and catarrh.

• Coriander is an excellent antispasmodic and digestive, stimulating appetite and enhancing absorption. An infusion of crushed seeds helps to relieve nausea, colic and heartburn. The seeds are often combined with laxatives to prevent any griping they may cause.

• Both leaf and seed are relaxing and can relieve stress-induced headaches and digestive disorders, including gastritis and peptic ulcers.

• The relaxant effect of coriander helps to relieve period pains; the ancient Arabs used it to lessen the pain of childbirth.

*Cross references*
peruvian pain killer, p. 82
cabbage and coriander syrup, p. 85
roman relief, p. 89

# barley _Hordeum vulgare_

> _"Barley water and other things made thereof do give nourishment to persons troubled with fevers, agues and heats in the stomach."_
>
> Nicholas Culpeper, 17th-century English herbalist

This unassuming grain has a great power to impart strength and replenish energy. It is very nutritious and easily digested, containing plenty of calcium, potassium, protein, and vitamins B complex and E. It relieves soreness and inflammation throughout the respiratory, digestive and urinary systems.

The physicians of ancient Greece and Rome recognized barley's soothing effect in relieving inflamed conditions of the digestive tract and its nutritious benefits in enhancing potency and vigour. Barley water and gruel were popular with the Victorian English who used them in the sick room during illness, fevers and convalescence to speed recovery and renew the patient's health and energy.

Barley water is an old European remedy for moistening the lungs, for sore, irritated conditions of the chest and harsh, dry and tickly coughs. It also makes an excellent remedy for soothing cystitis. Barley soup and gruel are good for combating wind and colic, diarrhoea as well as constipation, and for a weak digestion and a poor appetite. In a traditional English recipe barley was cooked with raisins, currants or prunes to make an energy-giving broth. In Holland it was cooked with buttermilk and sweetened with treacle to give to servants and children to maintain their strength.

Unrefined barley, known as pot barley and available in health food shops, is preferable to pearl barley, which has some of its outer layers removed and is not as nutritious. The outer husk is rich in substances that inhibit the synthesis of cholesterol by the liver, so it helps to lower cholesterol in the body.

## Healing qualities

• Nerve tonic to reduce stress and fatigue, relieve anxiety and lift the spirits. An excellent food for convalescence to build up strength and energy.

• A soothing and anti-inflammatory remedy to help relieve conditions such as harsh dry or irritating coughs, gastritis, diverticulitis, ulcerative colitis and cystitis.

• Promotes heart function and helps stabilize blood pressure. Protects against heart and arterial disease.

• Contains substances known as protease inhibitors, which are believed to suppress cancer-causing agents in the digestive tract.

• A good remedy for diarrhoea and constipation and to re-establish a normal bacterial population of the gut – excellent after a course of antibiotics and for candidiasis.

_Cross references_
gladiators' gruel, p. 57
old english barley water, p. 122

# oats *Avena sativa*

Sweet and nutritive, oats are the perfect rejuvenating tonic. Rich in protein, minerals (including calcium, magnesium, potassium, silicon and iron) and vitamin A, they make a great energy food for physically active people and for anyone who is run down and tired. Oats provide the body-building nutrients for healthy bones and teeth in children, and make an excellent nerve tonic for those suffering from anxiety, depression and nervous exhaustion. The fibre in oats produces bulkier stools and speeds their passage through the bowels, making oats a good treatment for those suffering from constipation and haemorrhoids.

Oat drinks and gruel made with spices, lemon, sugar or even wine have been popular for centuries for strengthening the chronically sick, the elderly, those convalescing after illness, and for women after childbirth. Originally from Eastern and Southern Europe, oats were introduced to Britain during the Iron Age. In medieval England, monks made the roasted grains into a laxative drink to treat constipation. They were also prescribed for insomnia, loss of appetite and debility. In Renaissance Italy, oats, in the form of porridge, were eaten more than any other food; Leonardo da Vinci apparently loved oats. Oat tea gained a reputation in the early 20th century for helping addicts to give up opium and reduce cravings for cigarettes. Oats are used by herbalists today to help those withdrawing from tranquillizers and antidepressants. While being stimulating and energy-giving, they are also relaxing and aid sleep.

*Avena sativa*, the cultivated oat developed from wild oats, is available in health food shops in the form of oatmeal and rolled oats, and in every supermarket as porridge oats. You can drink them in decoctions, soups and as gruel. They are easily digested and can be taken as a soothing remedy for irritated conditions of the digestive tract such as irritable bowel syndrome, diverticulitis and gastritis.

*"Potage is made of the lyquor in whiche flesshe is sodden in, with puttyng to chopped herbes, and otemel and salt."*
Piers the Plowman, 12th century

## Healing qualities

• Fibre in oats significantly lowers blood cholesterol if eaten regularly and reduces high blood pressure, helping to combat cardiovascular disease.

• By reducing the time carcinogens and irritants are exposed to the bowel wall, oats may help protect against bowel cancer.

• Oats have a regulatory effect on hormones in the body, notably sex and thyroid hormones, so may help to reduce incidence of menstrual and gynaecological problems, as well as breast cancer.

• Their ability to lower blood sugar makes oats an excellent food for diabetics.

*Cross references*
traditional english oatmeal and
   prune congee, p. 54
old english oatmeal caudle, p. 68
scottish oatmeal and cinnamon
   mover, p. 115

# almond

*Prunus amygdalus* var. *dulcis*

The sweet almond is adored all over the world for its taste and versatility. The rich protein, oil, vitamin and mineral content of almonds makes them an ideal food for times of rapid growth in childhood and teenage, during busy and stressful times and in convalescence. The high amounts of potassium, calcium and magnesium nourish the heart and brain, and support the nervous system, enhancing mental alertness, concentration and memory, and minimizing the effects of stress. Their strengthening effect in the body is ideal for maximizing vitality in active and sporty people, for increasing stamina in those feeling tired and run down, and for increasing sexual energy.

A relative of the peach and the plum, the sweet almond tree is a native of the Eastern Mediterranean. The Romans grew almonds and ate salted almonds with their meals to prevent drunkenness. The Arabs discovered them when they conquered Persia and introduced them to areas that are now renowned for their almond desserts such as Sicily and Spain. In 16th-century Europe almonds became popular as a remedy for fevers and troublesome coughs as well as kidney stones. Meanwhile the Muslim Moghuls' love of almonds influenced the cuisine of India, and the Eastern tradition of eating almond sweetmeats and drinking almond milk derives from this time.

Almond milk (ground almonds mixed with water) makes a delicious substitute for cow's milk with soothing and anti-inflammatory effects throughout the body. In the digestive tract it can relieve heartburn and indigestion, in the respiratory tract it can allay harsh, irritating coughs and in the urinary system, it soothes irritation and cystitis. Almonds' relaxant action relieves tension and spasm in the body and can reduce colic, flatulence, croupy coughs and period pains. Care needs to be taken not to eat underripe almonds as they can contain compounds which produce hydrogen cyanide, a poisonous gas.

*"The oil newly pressed out of Sweet Almonds is a mitigator of pain and all manner of aches, therefore it is good in pleurisy and colic."*
John Gerard, 16th-century English apothecary

## Healing qualities

• Almonds contain mostly monounsaturated fats, which are effective at lowering harmful cholesterol, so can help to protect the heart and arteries from disease. Their vitamin E also aids the prevention of heart disease.

• Vitamins B and E and a host of minerals make almonds a valuable nerve tonic and brain food. Excellent for those under pressure, they help to relieve tension and anxiety, and ensure a restful sleep.

• Taken in drinks, particularly milk, almonds are easily digested and make a nutritious alternative for breast milk when weaning babies.

• Soothing and relaxant properties make almonds a good remedy for stress-related digestive problems, while their laxative effect helps relieve constipation.

• The vitamin E and calcium in almonds reduce the symptoms of menopause and help to prevent osteoporosis.

• Antioxidants selenium and vitamin E help to slow the aging process and protect against arthritis and heart disease.

*Cross references*
almond milk, p. 67
greek almond regulator, p. 101
american papaya and almond
  dream, p. 110
serenity smoothie, p. 135

# beetroot *Beta vulgaris*

This smooth-textured, succulent vegetable, with its gorgeous deep-red colour, is hard to beat as a highly nutritious tonic to the immune system. Rich in antioxidant vitamins A, B complex and C, folic acid and minerals (including magnesium, iron and phosphorus), it provides vital nutrients to aid recovery and repair and to ward off the ravages of the aging process. The wealth of easily assimilated sugars provide instant energy and account for beetroot's reputation as a revitalizer and rejuvenator. Similar in properties to spinach, the edible green leafy tops are rich in beta-carotene, folic acid, calcium and iron.

A native of Southern Europe, beetroot has been grown since Assyrian times and was prized as a nourishing vegetable by the ancient Greeks who gave it as an offering to their sun god, Apollo, at his temple at Delphi. The Romans valued beetroot as a remedy for fevers. In medieval England the juice of beetroot was recommended as an easily digested food for the aged, weak or infirm, while in Eastern Europe the roots were used to treat headache and toothache. In the 1950s the Hungarian doctor Alexander Ferenczi introduced a revolutionary new treatment for cancer using nothing but raw beetroot, apparently with amazing success.

With its sweet taste and velvety texture, beetroot juice is a delightful way to ward off colds and flu through the winter. Beetroot has great cleansing properties and, taken regularly, should soon have you looking and feeling your best. By stimulating liver, bowel and kidney functions, it enhances the elimination of toxins and wastes. It also stimulates the lymphatic system to support the cleansing work of the immune system. When made into drinks and soups such as the famous Russian borscht, beetroot acts as a good decongestant, helping to clear catarrh during colds, coughs and flu. Some people are unable to metabolize the red pigment in beetroot and so excrete it harmlessly in their urine and stools which turn pink.

*"The red beet is good to stay the bloody flux, women's courses and the whites, and to help the yellow jaundice. The juice of the root put into the nostrils, purges the head, the noise in the ears, and the toothache."*
Nicholas Culpeper, 17th-century English herbalist

## Healing qualities

- A mild laxative, beetroot can help to prevent and remedy constipation, diverticulitis and haemorrhoids.

- Recent research has indicated that beetroot's immune-enhancing properties and detoxifying action may be helpful in cancer prevention and treatment.

- Folic acid in beetroot leaves provides a vital nutrient for pregnant women.

- Being rich in potassium, vitamins and minerals, beetroot helps to regulate blood pressure and heartbeat, and to support the nervous system.

- Beetroot's soothing effect in the digestive tract can remedy indigestion, acidity, gastritis and heartburn.

- By facilitating digestion and absorption, beetroot relieves problems associated with stagnation of food and toxicity, such as skin problems, headaches and lethargy.

*Cross references*
beet borscht cocktail, p. 78
hungarian beetroot and carrot cleanser, p. 100
russian relief, p. 115

# apple *Malus communis*

The tangy, refreshing apple is rich in vitamins, minerals and trace elements. It aids digestion and helps regulate acidity in the stomach, and by promoting liver and bowel functions has a cleansing and detoxifying action in the body. Freshly squeezed apple juice, drunk regularly, will enhance your immunity to infection and through its antiviral action will help to keep colds, flu and other viruses such as herpes simplex at bay.

Apple's reputation as a panacea is well founded. For centuries, apples have been known to speed recovery after illness and to relieve fevers, catarrh, coughs, sinusitis, anaemia, anxiety and insomnia. The acids in apples help the digestion of protein and fats in heavy, fatty foods, which is why apples are traditionally eaten with rich foods such as pork and goose. They have a cooling effect in the body, great for relieving hot, inflammatory problems. For warding off winter ills this cooling action can be balanced by adding warming spices such as cloves and cinnamon to your apple drinks. It is said that apples dampen the appetite, which is a great bonus for dieters.

The Romans knew around 22 varieties of apples and today there are around 2,000. Make your drinks with eating apples rather than cookers to reduce the need for sugar. Freshly squeezed apple juice is delicious and combines well with other juiced fruit and vegetables. When cooked with spices such as ginger, cinnamon, cloves and cardamom, apples make delightful warming drinks for autumn and winter.

## Healing qualities

• Apples can relieve indigestion, acidity, gastritis, peptic ulcers and IBS, and have a beneficial effect on the liver. With their astringent action they help curb diarrhoea.

• The pectin in apples helps to bulk out stools making apples an effective laxative for constipation sufferers.

• Pectin also detoxifies – it binds with toxic metals such as mercury and lead in the body and carries them out via the bowels.

• By aiding elimination of excess fluid and toxins, apples make a good cleansing remedy for those suffering from gout, arthritis, fluid retention and skin problems, and may help ease the symptoms of a hangover.

• Apples help to regulate blood sugar levels and to make a good food for diabetics. They also help lower blood cholesterol and blood pressure.

*Cross references*
apple and apricot slimmer, p. 51
carrot and apple juice, p. 52
traditional english oatmeal and prune
   congee, p. 54
american fruit defence, p. 64
blackcurrant and apple rob, p. 87
french apple and cinnamon tea, p. 141

# cabbage *Brassica*

"Doctor of the poor" and "a gift from heaven" are eulogies from the days when the cabbage was recognized as a panacea for all ills. High in fibre, low in calories, rich in vitamin C and a good source of bioflavonoids, potassium, folic acid and the B vitamins, this vegetable has a wonderful ability to detoxify the body, cleanse the skin, renew energy and promote feelings of wellbeing.

Strange as it may seem, the ancient Egyptians built a temple to honour the cabbage. The Greeks went one step further and passed a law that made stealing cabbages a crime punishable by death. Pythagoras apparently promoted the practice of eating raw cabbages every day, particularly to cure nervous or mental disorders. Ancient cultures were also quick to discover the cabbage's welcome power to combat the debilitating effects of headaches and hangovers.

Juices or soups are the best way to sample the healing properties of cabbages, whether they are the green, white, red, Savoy or Chinese variety. Raw cabbage blended into a juice is very beneficial, particularly for peptic ulcers. The juice can generate intestinal gas, however, causing bloating or flatulence. Red cabbage has the most vitamin C, while Savoy is a richer source of beta-carotene, the precursor of vitamin A. Cabbage contains sulphur, a contributor to its characteristic smell during cooking. When putting cabbages into a soup, drop a piece of stale bread into the water to eliminate the smell. Add some lemon juice and an aromatic spice, such as cumin, to complement the cabbage flavour.

Only buy cabbages that look fresh with crisp leaves, firm heads and a good colour. Avoid any that have any wilted leaves, cracked heads or that seem to have signs of insect damage.

*"Last evening you were drinking deep*
*So now your head aches; go to sleep*
*Take some boiled cabbage when you awake*
*There's an end of your headache."*
Tsar Alexis of Russia (1629–70)

## Healing qualities

• Cabbage stimulates the immune system and the production of antibodies, and is an excellent remedy for fighting bacterial and viral infections, such as colds and flu.

• The sulphur content of cabbage is probably responsible for its antiseptic, antibiotic and disinfectant actions, particularly in the respiratory system.

• Raw cabbage juice promotes the healing of ulcers, both internally and externally. Mucilaginous substances protect the lining of the digestive tract from irritants, and an amino acid, methionine, promotes healing.

• Bioflavonoids and antioxidant vitamins A, C and E afford some protection against tissue damage, degenerative disease and premature aging from free radicals.

• Cabbage juice makes a soothing, antiseptic gargle for sore throats and a mouthwash for mouth ulcers.

*Cross references*
cabbage and carrot juice, p. 75
cabbage and coriander syrup, p. 85
cabbage cooler, p. 93
nettle and cabbage soup, p. 133

# cinnamon

*Cinnamomum zeylanicum*

This most delicious of spices is a wonderful strengthening tonic to warm and enliven body and mind. A perfect remedy for winter, cinnamon dispels all sorts of conditions associated with the cold – poor circulation, colds, coughs, fevers and catarrh – and makes you feel alive and alert. By invigorating the nervous system, cinnamon can improve resistance to the stresses of everyday life. While being the perfect remedy to lift fatigue and chase away lethargy and low spirits, cinnamon also reduces tension and anxiety. The essential oil in cinnamon is one of the strongest natural antiseptic agents known. Antibacterial, antiviral and antifungal properties make cinnamon an excellent medicine to prevent and resolve a whole range of chronic and acute infections. It can help significantly in the treatment of ME and is excellent for gastrointestinal infections – it has been shown to inhibit the growth of *E. coli* and typhoid bacilli. Eugenol in the oil acts as an anaesthetic and helps relieve pain, for example in arthritis, rheumatism, headaches and muscle pain.

Cinnamon is native to India and Sri Lanka, where it has been highly prized for thousands of years – at times it was more valuable than gold. In Ayurvedic medicine cinnamon is popular for disguising the taste of other more unpleasant brews, and as an expectorant and decongestant for colds, coughs and catarrh. It is also given to strengthen the heart, restore the weak and debilitated, and promote "*agni*" or digestive fire. The Crusaders brought cinnamon to Western Europe not only to flavour foods and medicines but also for perfumes and love potions. In medieval Europe cinnamon was highly recommended as an aphrodisiac as well as a remedy for coughs and sore throats.

A hot cup of sweet and exquisitely aromatic cinnamon tea is a great way to stimulate the circulation and cause sweating, thereby helping to resolve fevers, flu and other infections. Mixed with cardamom and honey, cinnamon tea formed the basis of a hot drink which was very popular with British colonials in India who added rum and lemon rind to make their favourite Anglo-Indian punch. A pinch of ground cinnamon in fruit drinks, particularly those with apple, will help to balance their otherwise rather cooling nature. Ground cinnamon in milk is an old English country cure for diarrhoea and dysentery. In smoothies, cinnamon helps to neutralize the mucus-forming properties of milk.

*"Take thou also unto thee principal spices, of pure myrrh 500 shekels, and of cinnamon half as much, even 250 shekels, and of sweet calamus 250 shekels ... and thou shalt make it an oil of holy ointment."*
Holy Bible, Exodus 30

## Healing qualities

• The antimicrobial properties of cinnamon make it an excellent remedy for gastrointestinal infections and a wide range of respiratory infections.

• By enhancing digestion and absorption, cinnamon helps to relieve indigestion, colic, nausea and wind. It has also been shown to protect against stomach ulcers.

• The astringent action of the tannins in cinnamon stems bleeding and resolves diarrhoea and catarrhal congestion.

• Antifungal properties help combat thrush and systemic candidiasis.

• A circulatory stimulant, cinnamon will relieve symptoms associated with cold.

• By enhancing the effectiveness of insulin, cinnamon may help prevent a decline in glucose tolerance that can predispose to adult-onset diabetes.

• Its relaxant and astringent actions in the uterus help to relieve painful and heavy periods. Its strengthening properties can improve libido and sexual performance.

*Cross references*
chinese cinnamon and ginseng
   preventative, p. 65
scottish oatmeal and cinnamon mover,
   p. 115
french apple and cinnamon tea, p. 141

# ginseng

*Panax schinseng* (Korean or Chinese ginseng)

Revered in the East in life and legend, ginseng is the best tonic for increasing energy and longevity. Over the past 50 years nearly 3,000 scientific studies have demonstrated that it has the amazing ability to increase resistance to mental and physical stress whether caused by extremes of temperature, excessive exertion, illness, hunger, mental strain or emotional problems. Ginseng has been described as an "adaptogen", a remedy that increases tolerance of adverse influences and has a normal-izing action in the body; while relaxing those feeling tense and anxious, it is stimulating to others who feel tired and lethargic.

To the Chinese, *Panax schinseng* is the "king of tonics", the best remedy for all symptoms associated with *chi* deficiency, such as weakness, debility or simply old age. In the 1960s, Russian researchers showed that Siberian ginseng, *Eleuthrococcus senticosus*, improved immunity, enhanced nerve function and mental performance, increased strength and appetite, and improved blood flow through the arteries and brain.

American ginseng, *Panax quinquefolius*, has been used by Native Americans for hundreds of years – the Seneca tribe gave it to the elderly, while the Penobscots prescribed it for increasing female fertility. Overall, American ginseng is more tranquillizing and cooling than *Panax schinseng*, although it still has a great application in relieving fatigue. It was valued specifically in America for treating tuberculosis and more generally can be used to strengthen someone in the aftermath of a high fever.

Ginseng root can be made into decoctions or into tonic wines and elixirs. It can be taken on a short-term basis, for 3-4 months, during a physically or mentally stressful period and also to speed recovery from illness or surgery. Ginseng can be taken over a longer period by the elderly to reduce the impact of the aging process. Despite being considered a panacea, ginseng is not universally applicable. It should be avoided in acute inflammatory conditions and bronchitis as it can aggravate the symptoms.

*"Ginseng quietens the spirits, stabilizes the soul, invigorates the body and prolongs life."*
Chinese medical text, Shen Nung, 20BC

## Healing qualities

• Enhances mental performance, sharpens memory and diminishes fatigue by increasing the efficiency of nerve impulses.

• Heightens physical perfor-mance by inhibiting the utilization of glycogen in skeletal muscle.

• Works with insulin to aid reduction of blood sugar, helpful to diabetics.

• Antidiuretic action decreases urine production.

• Increases white blood cell production and improves immunity to allergies and disease.

• Has a stimulatory action on sexual func-tion in men and women.

• Reduces depression of the bone marrow in those on anticancer drug regimes. Helps the liver to resist hepatotoxins and radiation.

• Antioxidants help to protect the body against the ravages of the aging process and degenerative disease.

*Cross references*
chinese cinnamon and ginseng preventative, p. 65
ginseng and cardamom brain tonic, p. 68

# cucumber *Cucumis melo, Cucumis sativus*

The juicy cucumber, with its wonderfully cooling and refreshing taste, contains plenty of nutrients, despite consisting of 96 per cent water. These include antioxidant vitamins A and C and minerals calcium, potassium, manganese and sulphur. The mineral content helps to prevent nails splitting and to maintain healthy hair, while the potassium helps to regulate blood pressure. With its low calorific value, cucumber makes an excellent food for slimmers, while its diuretic action can help weight loss when there is fluid retention.

Originally from the East, where for thousands of years its cooling and thirst-quenching properties have been invaluable in the heat, the cucumber was one of the first vegetables to be cultivated. Its medicinal properties have long been put to good use to remedy heat and inflammation in the body. In India cucumber is eaten to cool the stomach and balance hot, spicy meals. Cucumber juice and water were old European folk remedies to bring down a fever. Sometimes a cucumber was placed alongside a sick infant and the heat of the fever was said to be absorbed by the cucumber. Gerard, the 16th-century English herbalist, recommended cucumber for inflamed chest conditions, excess heat and inflammation in the stomach and bladder, and for inflammatory skin conditions. Despite this, he still said that cucumbers "filleth the veines with naughty cold humours".

Ideal on a hot summer's day, cucumber drinks will keep you cool and prevent conditions like prickly heat and urticaria. Cucumber juice can be made by placing slices of peeled cucumber in a bowl for a couple of hours and then pressing them through fine muslin. With yogurt and mint, cucumber is a delicious ingredient of cold summer soups and dishes that relieve heat in the digestive tract, heartburn and indigestion, and combat stomach and bowel infections including *E. coli*. To obtain maximum nutrition from cucumber it is best eaten with the skin.

*"Cold herbes in the garden
for agues that burn
that over strong heats to
good temper may turn."*
Tusser, 16th-century English agriculturist

## Healing qualities

• The cooling and cleansing properties of cucumber can help to clear inflammatory skin conditions such as eczema as well as inflammatory eye problems.

• Cucumber's diuretic action is helpful in bladder infections, such as cystitis, for flushing out bacteria which may adhere to the bladder walls. It also aids fluid retention and helps to prevent formation of stones and gravel.

• By aiding the elimination of toxins and uric acid via the kidneys and through its ability to cool heat and inflammation, cucumber makes a good remedy for arthritis and gout.

• The sterols contained in cucumber are thought to lower harmful cholesterol in the body.

*Cross references*
middle eastern relish, p. 64
beet borscht cocktail, p. 78
spanish gazpacho, p. 99
indian cucumber raita drink, p. 118
cold cucumber and mint soup, p. 137

# pear *Pyrus communis*

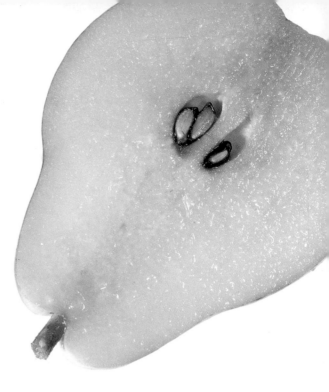

The sweet and juicy pear is a delicious source of fibre, vitamins, minerals and trace elements. Particularly when dried, pears are a good source of quick energy as they are high in natural sugars. They are low in substances that cause food allergies and so make an excellent food for allergy sufferers, especially those on exclusion diets. For this reason they make a good first food for babies when weaning.

A traditional European symbol of good health, fortune and hope, pears have been a popular food since Roman times. To the Chinese the pear represents longevity, justice and good judgement. Perry was invented in Roman times as an effective antidote to poisonous mushrooms. This delicious alcoholic "cure", made from a combination of wild and cultivated pears, was as popular a drink as cider in the 17th century. Gerard, the 16th-century English herbalist, wrote that perry "purgeth those that are not accustomed to drink thereof, especially when it is new – it comforteth and warmeth the stomach and causeth good digestion".

In Roman times there were apparently 39 varieties of pear, but today there are more than 3,000, which can be used interchangeably. Cooked or raw, their sweet subtle taste blends easily with other fruits and milks. Fresh pear juice is wonderfully refreshing and tastes like nectar. Like apples, pears have a cooling quality which can be offset in winter drinks by the addition of warming spices such as cinnamon, ginger and cloves. This ability to cool can be put to good use in relieving hot inflammatory conditions of the digestive tract and soothing an irritated bladder. Drinking three to six glasses of pear juice or pear water daily will help combat urinary infections, such as cystitis. To make pear water, heat 40-50g (1½-2oz) dried pears in 1.2 litres (2 pints) of water and simmer for half an hour.

*"All the sweet and luscious sorts, do help to move the belly downwards, more or less. Those that are hard and sour, do, on the contrary, bind the belly as much."*
Nicholas Culpeper, 17th-century
English herbalist

## Healing qualities

• The cooling and soothing action of pears quietens irritating coughs.

• Cooling qualities are beneficial for irritated and inflamed conditions of the digestive tract: heartburn, nervous dyspepsia, gastritis, IBS, colitis and diverticulitis.

• The pectin in pears provides fibre so can help regulate the bowels and relieve constipation and diarrhoea. Pectin also helps to reduce blood cholesterol levels.

• Diuretic action helps to eliminate toxins, aiding excretion of uric acid (helpful for gout sufferers) and fluid retention.

• Cooling and cleansing properties can help reduce heat and pain in arthritic joints.

• The boron in pears increases mental alertness and helps to prevent osteoporosis.

*Cross references*
thai tango, p. 49
caribbean calmer, p. 108
middle eastern pear and melon
 nectar, p. 111
chinese waterfall, p. 125

# garlic *Allium sativum*

If you need an invigorating tonic or even if you are looking for a rejuvenating elixir of youth, then garlic may well be your answer. This impressive bulb can impart energy and vitality, improve digestion and absorption and cleanse the body of toxins. It helps protect the body against the effects of pollution and nicotine. Acting as a powerful antioxidant, garlic helps to slow the aging process and protect against degenerative disease. Garlic is famous as a remedy for the heart and circulation, reducing blood pressure and a tendency to clotting, thus helping to prevent heart attacks and strokes.

The ancient Egyptians knew all about garlic's energy-giving properties, for the builders of the Great Pyramid at Giza apparently ate garlic to give them strength. The Romans, too, gave it to their workmen and soldiers to impart vigour as well as courage. To the Greeks garlic was a symbol of strength and athletes at the Olympic Games used to chew garlic before taking part to improve their chances of victory. Since such times until the present day garlic has been much valued for its great ability to ward off infection, to combat poisoning, diarrhoea, dysentery, wind and colic, and for diseases as serious as cholera and typhoid.

To some garlic's distinctive pungent taste is a delight while others malign it for its powerful and lingering odour. It can enliven a host of drinks including hot and cold soups and vegetable juices, and makes a great flavouring in sauces and dips. While doing so it invigorates the digestion, stimulating the secretion of enzymes and bile and enhancing the absorption of nutrients and thereby increases general health and vitality. It could well be its powerful antiseptic effect or its sometimes overpowering imprint on the breath that has given garlic a reputation for warding off evil, even vampires.

## Healing qualities

• An effective antibacterial, antiviral, antifungal and antiparisitic remedy, shown to be equal to antibiotics such as penicillin.

• Excreted via the lungs, the bowels, the skin and the urinary system, it disinfects each system as it goes.

• Excellent for sore throats, coughs, colds, flu, bronchitis and asthma. Helps to clear catarrh, sinus congestion and hay fever.

• Helps to re-establish beneficial bacterial population in the gut after an infection or using antibiotics; a good remedy for candidiasis and thrush.

• By enhancing the secretion of insulin, can help lower blood sugar in diabetics.

• The sulphur compounds in garlic are thought to have anti-tumour properties protecting the body against cancer.

• By stimulating the circulation garlic can relieve cramps and circulatory disorders.

• Regular intake of garlic may significantly lower harmful cholesterol and thereby protect against heart and arterial disease.

*Cross references*
italian tomato and thyme soup, p. 59
greek skorthalia, p. 63
middle eastern relish, p. 64
french garlic soup, p. 98
french garlic syrup, p. 119

# apricot *Prunus armeniaca*

The sweet-tasting, richly coloured apricot is said to have gained a place in the Garden of Eden through its beauty. John Ruskin, the 19th-century English social reformer, described it as "shining in sweet brightness of golden velvet". It is a nutrient-rich food, high in antioxidant vitamins A, B and C, and minerals including calcium, magnesium, potassium and iron (the iron content is highest in dried apricots; the vitamin C acts to enhance iron absorption). Since they are easily digested, apricot drinks are particularly good for anyone who is physically or mentally debilitated, anaemic or recovering from illness or stress. Calcium, magnesium and potassium are all essential for normal function of the nerves and the muscular system, and help to support the body through times of stress.

The apricot is a native of Central Asia and has been known in China for at least 2,000 years. It was brought to Europe by the Roman Lucullus after his campaigns in the East, to grow in his luxuriant gardens. It became popular as a delicacy and as a medicine for earache, nasal infections and haemorrhoids. Apricots were introduced to Britain in the 16th century and were used as a laxative.

The natural sweetness and blandness of apricots blend well with many other foods, making them very versatile and reducing the need for additional sweeteners. While being high in fibre, apricots are low in calories so they are good for anyone watching their weight. Drinks containing apricots have a wonderfully soothing effect throughout the digestive tract, calming irritation yet stimulating digestion and aiding the absorption of nutrients.

Apricots can cause allergic responses in some people as they contain salicylates. The sulphur used to preserve dried apricots can also cause allergic reactions so it is always best to buy unsulphured dried apricots.

*"The fruit thereof being taken after meat, do corrupt and putrifie in the stomacke; being first eaten before meat they easily descend and cause other meats to pass down the sooner."*
John Gerard, 16th-century English apothecary

## Healing qualities

• By preventing and relieving constipation, apricots help to protect against bowel disease including diverticulitis.

• The antioxidant vitamins A and C prevent damage caused by free radicals and help protect against heart and arterial diseases. They also act to slow the aging process and the onset of degenerative disease such as arthritis.

• The beta-carotene in apricots has been shown to protect against cancer of the lung and possibly the pancreas, the skin and the larynx, or any cancer linked to cigarette smoking.

• By providing nutrients for the nervous system, apricots can improve resilience to stress and can be used as a remedy for anxiety, tension, depression and insomnia.

• Their nourishing and strengthening effects on the body make apricots an excellent food for anyone feeling tired and run down, and for anyone with an increased need for easily absorbed nutrients such as pregnant women, children and the elderly.

*Cross references*
apple and apricot slimmer, p. 51
ginger cordial, p. 58
chinese apricot and grapefruit tonic, p. 95
american papaya and almond
   dream, p. 110

# cayenne *Capsicum annuum*

This hot, spicy pepper is famous the world over for its revitalizing and uplifting effect on mind and body. Its pungency, attributed to the presence of the alkaloid capsaicin, has a beneficial effect that permeates the body. The burning sensation on the tongue triggers the secretion of endorphins, opiate-like substances that can not only block pain but also induce a feeling of wellbeing, sometimes even euphoria. Cayenne improves digestion and absorption of nutrients, and by enhancing circulation ensures the transport of these nutrients to every tissue and the removal of waste products as well. Being rich in antioxidants beta-carotene, vitamin C and bioflavonoids, cayenne helps to slow the aging process and to protect against degenerative disease, cancer, and cardiovascular disease such as atherosclerosis and angina.

Like other varieties of pepper, cayenne derives from the same wild species that originated in Central and South America and was grown in Mexico as far back as 7000BC. Pre-Columbian ceramics decorated with peppers suggest the Aztecs were fond of them and cultivated them widely. Peppers were well respected as a medicine to strengthen the body against infection and to combat intestinal parasites. They were believed to have rejuvenating powers and were eaten for their aphrodisiac properties and to remedy infertility. Christopher Columbus was apparently responsible for their arrival in Europe – he believed he had found an alternative to the expensive black pepper.

Perfect for a cold winter's day, cayenne added to soups, teas and vegetable juices will stimulate the heart and circulation and warm you from the inside out. It is an excellent remedy for people prone to poor circulation and the problems that accompany it, including chilblains, cold extremities, lethargy and depression. By encouraging blood flow to the head, cayenne makes a good brain tonic, recommended for students to improve memory and concentration and for the elderly to ward off senility. Taken in a hot drink at the onset of a cold, flu or a fever, cayenne increases sweating and enhances the function of the immune system. If you find cayenne hard to swallow, start with small amounts and gradually build up a tolerance. It is best avoided by those prone to overheating and acidity of the stomach as it may aggravate the problems.

*"The greedy merchants, led by lucre, run
To the parched Indies and the rising Sun;
From thence hot pepper and rich drugs
    they bear,
Bartering for spices their Italian ware."*
John Dryden, 17th-century English poet

## Healing qualities

• Cayenne has a bactericidal action and is rich in vitamin C, making it a good remedy for the respiratory system.

• Cayenne's pungency acts as a quick and effective decongestant in the chest and upper respiratory tract, easing expectoration and relieving catarrh and sinusitis.

• Research shows that cayenne reduces irritation and broncho-constriction caused by inhaling cigarette smoke and pollutants.

• Cayenne's analgesic effect can be used to relieve the pain of toothache, shingles, arthritis and migraine.

• Through its warming action, cayenne can relieve symptoms caused by a weak or sluggish digestion, such as wind, nausea, diarrhoea, indigestion and abdominal pain.

• By relaxing spasm caused by poor circulation to and from the reproductive system, cayenne can help to prevent and relieve period pains.

• Cayenne has the ability to lower harmful cholesterol levels. It also may help to reduce blood pressure and prevent blood clots, strokes and heart attacks.

*Cross references*
watercress, spinach and tomato
    pick-me-up, p. 94
italian tomato juice, p. 140
caribbean lime and cayenne syrup, p. 144

# ginger *Zingiber officinale*

According to the Koran the menu served in Paradise includes ginger and certainly this most versatile of spices can impart a heavenly pungent flavour to a whole range of foods and drinks. Its warming and stimulating effects benefit the whole body, enhancing general health and vitality and dispelling the cold and lethargy that can permeate us on winter days.

Confucius wrote about ginger as early as 500BC, and soon after the spice appears in many prescriptions in Chinese medical texts. The Chinese valued it as a remedy for a whole variety of symptoms associated with cold and poor circulation, to strengthen the heart and sight, and as an aphrodisiac. In the Ayurvedic tradition of India ginger is known as "*vishwabhesaj*", the universal medicine, recognized not only for its ability to invigorate the body but also to enhance clarity in the mind, intelligence and determination. Medieval Italians considered ginger vital in prescriptions to promote a happy life in later years, by adding spice to their sex lives. A veritable rejuvenator! Recent research has shown that ginger inhibits clotting, thins the blood, lowers harmful blood cholesterol and reduces blood pressure.

Root ginger makes a delicious hot tea on its own, which is very effective when taken at the onset of a sore throat, cold or flu – when you feel tired, chilly and achy – to speed the infection on its way. The volatile oils in ginger are highly antiseptic, activating immunity and dispelling bacterial and viral infections. In India fresh ginger tea is given to children with whooping cough. Combined in teas with other spices such as cinnamon and cardamom, ginger is excellent as a winter warmer as it stimulates the heart and circulation throughout the body. It combines well with fruits, especially apples since it neutralizes their cold qualities. Ground ginger makes a good embellishment to many milk and fruit drinks.

*"Eat ginger and you will love and be loved as in your youth."*
Saying at the Salerno medical school, Italy, 11th century

## Healing qualities

• Enhances appetite and digestion by stimulating the flow of digestive juices.

• It relieves spasm and colic by relaxing the gut and makes an excellent remedy for bowel disorders, such as spastic colon, and nausea and vomiting caused by overeating, infection, travel sickness or pregnancy.

• Fresh root ginger is used in China to treat acute bacterial dysentery and makes a good remedy for all stomach and bowel infections.

• Ginger makes a good decongestant for catarrh and sinusitis, and an expectorant for coughs and chest infections.

• It relieves headaches, migraines and painful periods, and is able to invigorate the reproductive system in men and women alike, to increase libido and treat impotence.

• Ginger has antioxidant properties inhibiting free radicals and reducing the progress of the aging process.

### Cross references
ginger cordial, p. 58
malaysian ginger and lemon tea, p. 63
chinese ginger and fennel congee, p. 113
ginger beer, p. 117
medieval ginger cordial, p. 144

# sweet basil _Ocimum basilicum_

While flavouring your drinks with the most delicious of herbs, sweet basil will provide a tonic for the nervous system, an antiseptic for colds and flu and a relaxing remedy for the digestive system. Sweet basil helps calm the nerves, relieve tension, clear and stimulate the mind and lift the spirits. It is both reviving when you are tired and calming when feeling tense or anxious. It can help a variety of stress-related symptoms, including headaches, nerve pain and digestive disorders.

Taken in hot soups and teas, basil can clear catarrh in the nose and chest, relieve fevers, colds and coughs, and assist the body's fight against infection.

A native of India, sweet basil is traditionally planted near houses and on window ledges to purify the air and is revered for its _sattvic_ ability to clear the mind and open the heart. In many parts of the world, sweet basil has been valued for centuries for its ability to protect against infection and its strengthening properties have been associated with giving courage in times of difficulty. Romans used it as a tranquillizer and the Greeks still carry it with them to ensure a safe journey.

Basil is delightful in tomato soups and juices, as pistou, or as an addition to vegetable soups and in hot infusions. Green-leaved varieties, such as Italian, Albahaca and lettuce leaf, have similar healing properties to the purple-leaved "dark opal" and "purple ruffles", and they can be used interchangeably. However, they differ considerably in taste from Holy basil (_Ocimum sanctum_) and East Indian basil (_Ocimum gratissimum_). It is highly recommended to use fresh basil whenever possible for it loses much of its delicate pungent taste for which it is so popular when dried.

_"The smell of basil is good for the heart – it taketh away sorrowfulness, which cometh of melancholy and maketh man merry and glad."_
John Gerard, 16th-century English apothecary

## Healing qualities

• A good decongestant for colds, catarrh and sinusitis.

• An effective expectorant for coughs and a bronchial relaxant for croupy coughs and asthma.

• An immune enhancer and antiseptic to aid the body's fight against infection and intestinal parasites.

• A nerve tonic to strengthen the nerves, relieve depression and anxiety, improve concentration and sharpen the memory.

• A good remedy for pain relief, for headaches and migraine, back pain, muscle tension and rheumatism.

• A relaxing remedy for the digestion, for relieving wind, cramps, bloating, diarrhoea, constipation, nausea and indigestion.

_Cross references_
mediterranean magic, p. 83
spanish gazpacho, p. 99
italian potato, tomato and
   basil soup, p. 131

# rosemary *Rosmarinus officinalis*

Rosemary's detoxifying action on the liver cleanses the system and leaves you feeling brighter and healthier, rather like a good spring clean. Invigorating to mind and body alike, rosemary can help dispel lethargy and malaise, lift the spirits and improve memory and concentration. Its penetrating pine-like taste, delicious in aperitifs and digestives, stimulates the appetite, aids the digestion and absorption of nutrients, and is particularly good when eating fatty foods.

The ancient Greeks were well aware of rosemary's ability to keep the mind alert. Students revising for exams wore wreaths of rosemary around their heads to help them remember what they learned, and centuries later Shakespeare knew of rosemary's reputation when he had Ophelia say in Hamlet, "Here's rosemary for remembrance – I pray you love, remember". Since the days of the ancient Egyptians rosemary's association with remembrance has been linked to love and fidelity, in this world and in the afterlife. It was woven into posies and veils for weddings and held by mourners at funerals for it was even said to protect the soul from evil through eternity.

A steaming cup of rosemary tea makes a wonderful start to a winter's morning. By stimulating the circulation rosemary will warm you from the top of your head to the tips of your toes. This is a great way to throw off early morning stupor and yet rosemary's calming effects will help guard against the stresses of the day, relieve tension and anxiety, and lift tiredness and depression. It is also worth trying for a hangover. Being rich in calcium, rosemary is a wonderful medicine for the nerves. Whether in teas, soups or cordials, rosemary is probably most famous as a remedy for headaches and migraines. By stimulating blood flow to the head, relaxing tense muscles, aiding digestion and cleansing the liver, rosemary can provide relief for headaches from a variety of different causes.

*"The spirits of the heart and entire body feel joy from this drink which dispels all despondency and worry."*
Wilhelm Ryff, Renaissance herbalist of Strasburg

## Healing qualities

• Antibacterial, antiviral and antifungal properties boost the function of the immune system in warding off infection.

• In hot tea rosemary helps to chase away sore throats, colds, flu, fevers and chest infections. It can also help relieve tight coughs, wheezing and asthma.

• By stimulating the circulation, rosemary can be used for chilblains, varicose veins and haemorrhoids.

• Its diuretic action aids the elimination of toxins and excess fluid.

• Its detoxifying action can help clear wastes from the system and help relieve arthritis, gout and skin problems.

• With its astringent tannins, rosemary checks bleeding, reduces excessive menstruation and tones the digestive tract.

• A muscle relaxant, rosemary can reduce period pains and relieve wind and colic.

• Can help to slow the aging process and guard against degenerative disease.

***Cross references***
mediterranean make-over, p. 61
carrot and rosemary juice, p. 83
elizabethan rosemary and
   lemon syrup, p. 89
french onion soup, p. 97

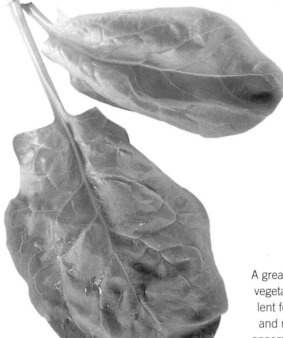

# spinach *Spinacia oleracea*

A great strengthening and energizing vegetable, spinach makes an excellent food for anyone feeling tired and run down, and for the anaemic and elderly. A storehouse of nutrients, it contains vitamins and minerals, including vitamins C and E, beta-carotene, iron, folic acid, potassium, calcium, magnesium and chlorophyll. Spinach has the bonus of being easy to digest and, in fact, has digestive properties itself, enhancing appetite and stimulating digestion and absorption by increasing the secretion of digestive enzymes and bile. A perfect tonic.

Spinach is thought to have originated in South-West Asia or the Western Himalayas, and was first cultivated in Persia. The early Arabs apparently prized it as a dish of great distinction and took it to Spain in the 10th century, from where its popularity spread to the rest of Europe. It was grown by monks in many medieval monasteries in Europe and formed part of a peasant's diet at that time. In 16th-century England it became popular as a light, nutritious and easily digested vegetable. It was given to convalescents and the weak and infirm to impart vigour and strength and to help restore them to health. In the early 20th century spinach was considered an excellent food not only for anaemia and lassitude, but also for kidney and heart problems, indigestion, piles and constipation.

Spinach is delicious in soups and vegetable dishes, imparting a rich, tangy flavour and vibrant dark-green colour that almost makes you feel better just looking at it. The abundant chlorophyll and bioflavonoids that give spinach its wonderful hue are also greatly therapeutic. Taken regularly, they are believed to help deactivate carcinogens in the body and so may inhibit tumour formation. Among the bioflavonoids are the carotenoids beta-carotene and lutein, which have both been shown to help prevent cancer of the colon, stomach, lungs and the prostate. It is said that of all vegetable juices, spinach may be the best for cancer prevention. Due to its high oxalic acid content, spinach is best avoided by anyone who suffers from gout, arthritis or kidney or bladder stones.

*"Being boiled to pulp and without other water than its own moisture, [spinach] is a most excellent condiment with butter, vinegar, or lemon, for almost all sorts of boiled flesh, and may accompany a sick man's diet. 'Tis laxative and emollient, and therefore profitable for the aged."*
John Evelyn, 17th-century English diarist

## Healing qualities

• Spinach's mild laxative action helps to clear wastes from the bowel and prevent constipation and diverticulitis.

• The fibre in spinach helps to lower harmful cholesterol levels and so protects against heart and circulatory problems.

• Aids the elimination of toxins via the kidneys, so it can be valuable in treating health problems associated with toxicity, including skin disease.

• Enhances immunity and so helps the body fight off infection.

• Antioxidants help to ward off degenerative disease including arthritis and heart disease.

• The folic acid in spinach helps to prevent anaemia. It is also vital for pregnant women to ensure normal development of the baby's brain and spinal cord.

• The carotenoids in spinach have been found to help protect eyesight by protecting against macular degeneration, the most common cause of blindness in people over the age of 65.

*Cross references*
canton watercress and spinach soup, p. 53
trinidadian spinach soup, p. 62
watercress, spinach and tomato
  pick-me-up, p. 94

# thyme *Thymus vulgaris*

Warming, stimulating and with its piquant flavour, thyme exhilarates mind and body alike. It enhances immunity and helps the body to throw off infections such as colds, coughs and flu. Its beneficial effect on the nervous system is excellent for physical and mental exhaustion, and for relieving tension, anxiety and depression.

To the Greeks thyme was an emblem of action and bravery, to the Romans a cure for melancholy. To others, it is a herb to quell fears and nightmares. Made into a soup, it was a medieval cure for shyness. In 14th-century England, ladies would embroider a bee hovering over a sprig of thyme on scarves to give to their knights as they went off into battle, to lend them courage. In those days thyme was also prized for its ability to strengthen the brain and increase longevity. Modern science has provided us with a good explanation for this. Thyme acts as an antioxidant, protecting against the harmful effects of free radicals, and thereby helps slow the onset of the aging process and degenerative disease.

Made into tisanes or sweet-tasting syrups that children will relish, thyme provides an excellent antiseptic remedy to ward off infections and relieve fevers. As a flavouring in soups and a garnish to fresh vegetable juices, such as tomato juice, thyme makes a good digestive, enhancing digestion and absorption, and helping to prevent problems such as wind, colic and indigestion. By stimulating the circulation, thyme is warming and strengthening, enhancing overall health and vitality. Its special affinity for the reproductive system means that both men and women might find that drinking thyme tea could improve their sex life.

> *"It is a noble strengthener of the lungs, as notable as one as grows; neither is there scarce a better remedy growing for that disease in children which they commonly call the Chin-cough, than it is."*
> Nicholas Culpeper, 17th-century English herbalist

## Healing qualities

• An excellent remedy for all kinds of respiratory infections, sore throats, colds, coughs and flu. As an expectorant it clears congestion from the bronchial tubes, while its relaxant properties relieve harsh, irritating coughs and asthma.

• Thyme relaxes spasm in the gut, relieves wind and colic, IBS and spastic colon. A good astringent remedy for diarrhoea and antiseptic for infections.

• By helping to re-establish a normal bacterial population of the bowel thyme is good for people taking antibiotics and with systemic candidiasis.

• With its antiseptic and diuretic action, thyme is good for urinary infections, rheumatism, gout and fluid retention.

• Thyme has a regulatory effect in the female reproductive system, relieving period pains and treating infections. It makes a good remedy for thrush.

### Cross references
italian tomato and thyme soup, p. 59
greek thyme tea, p. 65
thyme syrup, p. 75
greek sage and thyme infusion, p. 77

# watercress _Nasturtium officinale_

Dark green with a fresh, peppery taste, watercress makes an excellent tonic and cleanser of the blood. Rich in vitamins A, C and E, it is a good source of calcium, iron, potassium, zinc and trace elements. Bitter and pungent at the same time, watercress makes a tasty and nourishing soup that warms the body, stimulates the circulation, restores energy and can help cleanse the body of toxins. It is an excellent blood cleanser, detoxifier and nourishing tonic.

Twice daily doses of watercress juice apparently increased the productivity of the slaves of ancient Egyptian kings. In Greece, Hippocrates, the father of medicine, recommended it as a stimulant; Dioscorides believed it had aphrodisiac powers; and Xenophon suggested that feeding children on watercress would give them firm, healthy bodies. The fact that watercress made people feel so well gave it a mystical reputation: not only could it draw from the earth those elements vital for health, but it also conferred intelligence on those who ate it.

Watercress soup, juice or tea are essential to the healing armoury of any kitchen. Bunches of watercress – there are no varieties – are usually available throughout the year. Choose bunches with bright green leaves and avoid those with yellow or wilting leaves, and those that are in flower. Do not pick watercress growing in streams or ponds, especially near sheep pastures, which may be contaminated by parasites, such as liver flukes, or bacteria that can cause intestinal problems.

_"Eat watercress often to have a sharpe and ready wit."_
_Practitioner in Physicke_, William Langham, 1579

## Healing qualities

• An effective antiseptic, watercress is particularly good for chest infections as it acts as a respiratory stimulant and expectorant. It can help relieve bronchitis, pleurisy, pneumonia and tuberculosis.

• Watercress invigorates the digestion, improves the appetite and provides a great tonic for food stagnation, poor absorption, wind, colic and worms.

• Watercress can act on the kidneys and bladder, increasing the flow of urine and dissolving stones and gravel.

• Its blood-cleansing properties bring symptomatic relief to sufferers of arthritis, rheumatism and gout.

• Watercress stimulates the circulation, encouraging absorbed nutrients to reach the parts of the body where they are most needed, and giving a sense of physical wellbeing and strength.

• Its vitamin E content is useful in the prevention and treatment of premenstrual syndrome and is believed to enhance fertility, increase sexual energy, cure impotence and stimulate menstrual flow and lactation.

_Cross references_
canton watercress and
    spinach soup, p. 53
watercress soup, p. 60
watercress, spinach and tomato
    pick-me-up, p. 94
french potassium juice, p. 124

# yogurt

Astonishingly beneficial for the digestive system, yogurt, eaten regularly, will improve your health and may even make you live longer. Yogurt is sour, fermented milk, curdled to a custard-like consistency by the action of bacteria which produce lactic acid. Live yogurt contains some notable bacteria, namely *Lactobacillus bulgaricus* and *L. acidophilus*, which are able to survive the process of digestion. In the bowel, they re-establish the normal bacterial population and eliminate an overgrowth of harmful bacteria caused by unhealthy diets, being run down or the use of antibiotics. Lactic acid in yogurt has the additional benefits of aiding the synthesis of B vitamins and increasing the absorption of nutrients such as calcium and iron. It also regulates bowel function and inhibits infections.

An angel is said to have revealed to Abraham in the Bible the life-giving properties of yogurt, which accounted for his longevity. These amazing qualities were rediscovered in the early 1900s by Russian scientist and Nobel prize winner Dr Elias Metchinikoff. He propounded that much disease is related to putrefactive bacteria in the bowel. Having found that these destructive microbes could be checked by other micro-organisms in yogurt, he set out to prove the relationship between eating yogurt and longevity. Tales of extraordinary longevity in parts of Africa, America and Bulgaria – where people whose staple diet was yogurt lived longer than any others in Europe – corroborated Metchinikoff's theory.

Yogurt has since been the subject of extensive research. Recent studies indicate that an acidophilus culture – one of the natural antibiotics contained in live yogurt – can help suppress the activity of enzymes in the colon that convert certain chemicals into carcinogens, suggesting that yogurt may be beneficial in preventing cancer.

Yogurt made from cow's, goat's or sheep's milk lends a creamy texture to drinks and is delicious with herbs such as mint and dill. Its cooling properties are a bonus in hot weather and when eating a hot curry.

*"Usefulness: Against swellings of the stomach.
Effects: It generates phlegmatic blood. It is
suitable for warm temperaments, for young people,
in summer, and in southerly regions."*
*Tacuinum sanitatis*, medieval health handbook

## Healing qualities

• Good for relieving wind, abdominal pain, constipation and IBS. Combats allergies and candidiasis.

• Regulates bowel function and inhibits infections such as *E. coli*. Good for helping to prevent travellers unaccustomed to foreign bacteria from succumbing to infection. Also prevents bladder infections and cystilis.

• Acts as an immune enhancer, increasing general resistance to infection.

• Yogurt's soothing effect on the digestive tract can help relieve heartburn.

• Contains prostaglandins which help protect the stomach lining against irritants such as alcohol and cigarette smoke, and may reduce the incidence of peptic ulcers.

• Said to protect against heart disease by increasing high-density lipoprotein cholesterol in the body and lowering harmful cholesterol.

• Has a reputation for keeping the mind alert and warding off senility.

***Cross references***
indian sweet lassi, p. 104
russian relief, p. 115
indian cucumber raita drink, p. 118
cold cucumber and mint soup, p. 137

2

drinks for looking good, feeling good

# drinks for looking good, feeling good

Positive health is the goal of this book, not simply keeping yourself free from illness, but unmistakably looking and feeling your best. Your skin should not only be clear of spots and blemishes but have a lustre and glow that is an outward sign that all is well within. Similarly your hair should shine, your eyes look clear and sparkling. Your body should move with energy and ease. These are the physical manifestations that can only exist if they mirror the wellbeing and vitality that we feel inside.

Such a balanced state of health and vitality depends on many factors. Our diet needs to be abundant in nutrients to provide us with all the raw materials for the maintenance of every vital function of the body. Each system needs to be provided for. Our nervous systems, for example, require sufficient vitamin B and C, calcium, magnesium and essential fatty acids to ensure that we cope with the stress in our lives and keep a balanced perspective. Our immune systems, vital for prevention of and recovery from infection and problems of immunity including cancer, need nutrients such as vitamins A, B, C and E, calcium, magnesium, iron, zinc and selenium.

Our digestions need to be robust and efficient enough to break down, absorb and assimilate these nutrients. They also need to excrete the waste products of their metabolism effectively so that we remain free from an over-accumulation of toxins that make us feel off-colour and lethargic and contribute to disease. We also need to try to lead a lifestyle that is as stress-free and conducive to health and wellbeing as it possibly can be. We need to balance the activity of each day with periods of rest and relaxation and get plenty of sleep to replenish our batteries. We also need to take adequate exercise on a regular basis to ensure good circulation of blood to and from every cell and tissue in the body. Only this way will each cell receive the oxygen and nutrition it needs to function at its best and be relieved of wastes and toxins.

The amazing health giving properties of fresh foodstuffs can be put to excellent use by their daily inclusion in drinks that are not only quick but also easy to make. Good, healthy food may already figure to some extent in our regular meals but it is never easy to balance our daily requirements of nutrients with our intake and many of us resort to supplements because we feel or look tired and run down. The drinks that follow are abundant in a whole range of nourishing ingredients that, if drunk regularly, will soon have you looking and feeling radiant.

# losing weight

Our weight is closely connected with our health in every sense, for being overweight not only affects how we feel about ourselves, our confidence and positivity but also contributes to a range of health problems, including diabetes, high blood pressure and heart disease.

The main concerns when losing weight are to reduce the amount of calories you take in, increase the amount you expend and ensure that your body processes what you eat and drink properly. Combining healthy eating with regular exercise will not only decrease your weight but also increase your energy, vitality and *joie de vivre*. You need to take 20-30 minutes of continual aerobic exercise a day, such as swimming, bicycling, brisk walking, jogging or dancing.

The best way to lose weight is slowly and naturally – about 1-1.5kg (2-3lb) a week is ideal. This can be achieved by eating plenty of fresh fruit and vegetables, high fibre and unrefined carbohydrates and drinking plenty of liquid, with spices and herbs to flavour your food and drinks. Make sure that you eat regularly, three main meals a day (including one main protein meal), with a couple of snacks in between. Don't be tempted to deprive yourself, miss meals or go for long periods without eating, as this sends stress messages to the brain and will lead to overeating or binging on the wrong kinds of foods.

## jamaican grapefruit and pineapple spritz

This light, cooling and refreshing drink makes a great accompaniment to the hot spicy food that the Jamaicans love. Both grapefruit and pineapple are ideal foods for losing weight. They cleanse the urinary system and help the body to get rid of excess toxins and fluid, and also help the digestive system to break down fats. A further benefit brought by this delicious drink is that it clears putrefaction from the bowels and helps to remedy constipation.

*500ml (16fl oz) pink grapefruit juice or*
  *juice of 2 fresh grapefruit*
*250ml (8fl oz) pineapple juice*
*ice cubes*
*750ml (1¼ pints) sparkling mineral water*
*4 fresh pineapple slices*
*4 sprigs fresh mint*

Pour 125ml (4fl oz) of grapefruit juice and 60ml (2fl oz) of pineapple juice into each glass. Add a few ice cubes and fill up with mineral water. Garnish each drink with a pineapple slice and a sprig of mint. 4 servings

## russian asparagus soup

Wild asparagus covers the Tundra steppes in Russia where this rather luxurious soup is popular. It has a cleansing effect on the whole body and is particularly good for eliminating toxins and excess fluid through its stimulating effect on the kidneys. This is augmented by the beneficial action of asparagus on the liver and intestines, aiding digestion and preventing constipation. The mild taste of the succulent asparagus is brought to life by the aromatic dill leaf which is also a marvellous aid to digestion.

*2 tablespoons olive oil*
*1 onion, peeled and sliced*
*2 medium potatoes, peeled and diced*
*450g (1lb) asparagus, washed and chopped*
*1 litre (1¾ pints) water*
*salt and freshly ground pepper*
*2 tablespoons natural yogurt (optional)*
*2 tablespoons chopped fresh dill, to garnish*

Heat the oil in a saucepan and add the onion, potato and asparagus. Cover and cook over a low heat for 10 minutes, stirring occasionally. Add the water, bring to the boil and simmer for about 20 minutes, until the vegetables are soft. Blend and pass through a sieve to remove any fibrous bits. Season with salt and pepper and reheat. Swirl the yogurt (if using) into the soup and garnish with plenty of fresh dill. 4 servings

## thai tango

Almost a meal in itself, this exotic combination of tropical fruits makes a great way to start a summer's day. It is filling and yet slimming at the same time. The sweet juicy papaya is highly nutritious, packed with vitamin C and beta-carotene, and together with the pears provides a good source of fibre to ensure efficient bowels. Papaya also contains enzymes which are a great aid to digestion. The tangy lime adds bite, stimulates digestion and clears excess fluid from the body.

*100g (4oz) fresh papaya, sliced*
*juice of 1 lime*
*2 medium pears, peeled and sliced*
*200ml (7fl oz) rice milk*
*a pinch of ground ginger*
*ice cubes (optional)*

Combine all the ingredients and blend. For a long refreshing drink, pour over ice.
1 serving

## florence fennel and artichoke soup

This appetizing Italian soup marries the delicate flavour of artichoke and the distinctive aniseed taste of fennel. Artichoke water aids digestion of fats, through its stimulating effect on the liver, and by its diuretic action clears fluid and toxins from the system. Fennel, another wonderful digestive, combines diuretic action with laxative effects, making it a perfect friend to slimmers.

*2 globe artichokes*
*1.2 litres (2 pints) water*
*1 tablespoon olive oil*
*1 large onion, peeled and sliced*
*2 garlic cloves, peeled and chopped*
*2 medium potatoes, peeled and diced*
*2 bulbs fennel, sliced*
*1 teaspoon fennel seeds*
*salt and freshly ground pepper*
*fresh parsley, to garnish*

Place the artichokes in a pan with the water, bring to the boil and simmer for 20 minutes. Heat the oil in a pan and gently cook the onion, garlic and potatoes for 10 minutes. Add the fennel, fennel seeds and artichoke water and bring to the boil. Cover and simmer on a low heat for about 20 minutes, until the vegetables are cooked. Season to taste, blend and serve with a garnish of fresh parsley. 4 servings

## apple and apricot slimmer

A delectable smoothie for those watching their weight, this combination of sweet fruits and yogurt is almost a meal in itself. Apricots are high in fibre and low in calories and at the same time satisfy that urge to have something sweet. Apples aid digestion and absorption and have the ability to dampen the appetite, which is always a great bonus for weight watchers.

*6 dried apricots*
*125ml (4fl oz) apple juice*
*100g (4oz) natural live yogurt, low fat*
*a little freshly grated nutmeg*

Cook the apricots in a little water until soft then drain. Blend with the apple juice and yogurt and top with a sprinkling of nutmeg. 1 serving

## corfiot horta and rigani tea

Tender young dandelion leaves, known in Corfu as *horta*, are prized by the locals who regularly collect them from the wild to boil and eat like spinach. The water the leaves are cooked in is considered very healthy to drink and it certainly has a powerful diuretic effect. It tastes faintly bitter but when combined with the penetrating flavour of oregano (*rigani*) makes a light and refreshing tea, which doubles as a digestive when drunk after meals. This dynamic duo is recommended to those watching their weight for its combined effects of eliminating excess fluid and stimulating digestion.

*2 tablespoons young dandelion leaves,*
*   washed and chopped*
*2 teaspoons dried or 4 teaspoons*
*   fresh oregano*
*600ml (1 pint) boiling water*

Place the herbs in a teapot and pour over boiling water. Cover and leave to infuse for 10 minutes. Drink a cupful 3 times daily after meals. 2-3 servings

# clear eyes

The sparkle or lustre in the eyes tells us volumes about a person, whether they are happy or unhappy, if they sleep well or not and whether they are healthy or run down. While the condition of our eyes is closely linked to our general health and lifestyle, there is much we can do through our diet to keep our eyes healthy and help to prevent problems such as dry, inflamed eyes, swollen or puffy eyelids, blepharitis and cataracts.

Our mothers or grandmothers may well have persuaded us to eat up our carrots so that we could see in the dark and certainly they were right to do so. Carrots are very high in beta-carotene which is converted to vitamin A in the body, an essential nutrient for healthy eye tissue and good vision. Night blindness is more often than not caused by lack of vitamin A in the diet, and remedied simply by eating about three carrots a day. Beta-carotene, like vitamins C and E, folic acid and selenium, is an antioxidant, vital for protecting the body against damage caused by free radicals and thereby for maintaining the health of the eyes. It is also found in yellow- and orange-coloured fruit and vegetables, including apricots, mangoes, peppers, squashes and green leafy vegetables such as spinach and watercress.

Eating plenty of avocado and walnuts boosts our vitamin E intake and oily fish, linseed and evening primrose provide omega-3 essential fatty acids, both vital to the eyes and a deficiency of which can cause dry, gritty and red eyes, making you feel as well as look tired. Oranges, lemons, blackberries and blackcurrants, with lots of vitamin C, can all help to slow down the development of cataracts. So too can tea, onions and red wine, thanks to the quercetin they provide, and yeast extract, nuts, seeds and whole wheat with their vitamin B$_2$.

Blueberries, cranberries, citrus fruits, green leafy vegetables and red peppers are rich in flavonoids and vitamin C which help to maintain efficient circulation to and from the eyes and the strength of the capillaries, thereby helping to slow the deterioration of eyesight that accompanies the aging process. Such foods will also support the immune system and inhibit the kind of infection that causes problems such as styes and conjunctivitis.

## carrot and apple juice

The natural sweetness of both carrots and apples makes this a most palatable drink and one that is bursting with nutrients for the eyes, notably beta-carotene and vitamin C. It also makes a good aid to digestion and, by helping to keep the bowels regular, it clears toxins from the system, something that is vital to keep the eyes clear and healthy. The immune-enhancing properties of carrots and apples, together with the cooling effects of coriander, help to keep at bay allergies, infections and inflammations that contribute to eye problems such as conjunctivitis and styes.

*100ml (3½fl oz) carrot juice*
*100ml (3½fl oz) apple juice*
*fresh coriander leaves, to garnish*

Combine the juices and serve with a garnish of coriander leaves. 1 serving

## canton watercress and spinach soup

Packed with antioxidant vitamins, minerals and trace elements, this vibrant dark green soup provides vital nutrition for the health of the eyes. The cleansing properties of both watercress and spinach, through their diuretic and laxative actions, help to keep us in tip-top condition, not only feeling but also looking good. Watercress and spinach are popular among the Chinese for their cooling and moistening effects which help to clear dryness, heat and congestion that contribute to inflammatory and infectious eye problems.

*1 tablespoon olive oil*
*2 medium onions, peeled and sliced*
*3 medium potatoes, peeled and cubed*
*1 bunch watercress, washed and chopped*
*225g (8oz) spinach, washed*
*1.5 litres (2½ pints) water or vegetable or*
   *chicken stock*
*salt and freshly ground pepper*
*2 tablespoons fresh parsley or coriander*
   *or 1 tablespoon fresh thyme*
*125ml (4fl oz) natural yogurt, to garnish*
   *(optional)*

Heat the oil in a large pan. Cook the onion and potatoes for 5 minutes. Add the watercress and spinach and cook for a further 5 minutes. Cover with water or stock, bring to the boil gently and simmer for 30 minutes or until the potatoes are soft. Remove from the heat, blend and add seasoning. Garnish with fresh herbs and a swirl of yogurt when serving. 6 servings

## moroccan carrot soup

In the souks of Marrakesh you may find this exquisite blend of sweet young carrots and fresh mint, which not only delights your taste buds but also allows your eyes to take in the night life of Morocco to the full. The carrots and mint provide plenty of beta-carotene and vitamin C to keep the eyes healthy, while the warming spices ensure good circulation to the eyes and give extra sparkle.

*2 tablespoons olive oil*
*1 medium onion, peeled and sliced*
*1 tablespoon finely chopped fresh root ginger*
*1 teaspoon curry powder*
*50g (2oz) rice*
*1kg (2¼lb) carrots, washed and sliced*
*1 litre (1¾ pints) vegetable or chicken stock*
*salt and freshly ground pepper*
*2 tablespoons chopped fresh mint leaves,*
   *to garnish*

Heat the oil in a pan, add the onion and ginger and cook for a few minutes until the onion is soft. Add the curry powder and rice and stir over the heat for 1 minute. Add the carrots and stock, bring to the boil and simmer for about 20 minutes, until the rice and carrots are tender. Season to taste and blend. Garnish with mint when serving. 6 servings

# great skin

Your complexion reflects your inner state of health so it is important to get rid of toxins that congest the tissues and cause spots and blemishes. The Chinese make a simple delicious tea with luscious fresh cherries that is perfect to improve complexion. Rich in antioxidant vitamins A and C, as well as calcium, magnesium, potassium and iron, cherries nourish both skin and nerves, and help to keep you looking young. By assisting liver, kidney and bowel functions, they enhance the elimination of toxins.

Vitamin C builds collagen and elastin, which help to keep the skin free from wrinkles. Vitamin A keeps the skin supple, healthy and clear of spots, and ensures rapid healing. B vitamins help to balance the function of the skin as well as the nervous system, increasing resilience to stress.

## chinese cherry tea

*To the Chinese the delicate cherry blossom in spring is a symbol of youth, fertility and feminine beauty. Here, lemon juice boosts the vitamin C and the cleansing properties of the cherry, giving it a wonderful tang.*

1 tablespoon sugar-free cherry jam
1 teaspoon honey
2 teaspoons fresh lemon juice
300ml (½ pint) boiling water

Place the jam, honey and lemon juice in a jug. Add boiling water, stir and leave to infuse for 5 minutes. Drink hot.
1 serving

## leek and pea vichyssoise

*With its subtle green colour, this thick creamy soup will add elegance to any summer meal when eaten cold. You can also serve it hot in the winter. Vichyssoise actually originated in America but was developed at the Ritz Carlton in New York by a French chef called Louis Diat, who came from the spa town of Vichy. The combination of leeks and peas is ideal for providing a plentiful supply of nutrients for the skin as well as for ensuring elimination of toxins from the body to keep the skin clear.*

1 tablespoon olive oil
4 medium leeks, washed and
   sliced thinly
2 medium potatoes, peeled and
   diced
100g (4oz) peas
1 sprig mint
600ml (1 pint) chicken or vegetable
   stock
salt and freshly ground pepper
150ml (¼ pint) single cream
   or natural yogurt
chopped chives, to garnish

Heat the oil in a saucepan, add the leeks and potatoes and stir for 5-10 minutes. Add the peas, mint, stock and seasoning. Bring to the boil, cover and simmer on low heat for 15-20 minutes. When cool blend with the cream or yogurt. Serve with a garnish of fresh chives.
4 servings

## traditional english oatmeal and prune congee

*This thick oaty drink is a veritable tonic to the nerves, soothing away tension and banishing low spirits. One of the best ways to help your skin to stay young and healthy. Oat fibre speeds the passage of wastes through the gut while the prunes add their effective laxative properties to make this a nourishing yet cleansing drink to keep the skin clear of spots. The apple juice contributes further detoxifying actions by promoting liver and bowel function and through its diuretic effect.*

100g (4oz) dried prunes
900ml (1½ pints) water
50g (2oz) rolled oats
2 tablespoons honey
450ml (¾ pint) unsweetened
   apple juice

Place the prunes in water and simmer in a covered pan for 30 minutes until soft. Remove the stones and add the oats, stirring until the mixture comes to the boil. Cook, stirring all the time, for 5 minutes until thick. Stir in the honey and apple juice. Reheat and serve.
4 servings

# raising energy

A good supply of energy, though a vital requisite for a sense of health and wellbeing, is not necessarily easy to come by. Plenty of fresh air and exercise are essential – a brisk walk for half an hour once a day will be enough to stimulate your circulation, help alleviate stress and encourage a restful sleep.

Grains, vegetables and fruits provide the raw materials to nurture our bodies, build resilience to stress and ensure a plentiful supply of energy. A good digestive system will extract the nutrients you need and eliminate wastes – this is why soups based on these foods contain digestive herbs and spices, such as parsley, coriander, chives and thyme.

Delicious warming spices, such as ginger, cloves, cinnamon and cardamom, can quickly boost energy and vitality. By stimulating the circulation they enhance all the vital functions of the body, and also chase away feelings of tiredness and lethargy. Try ginger or cinnamon tea to ward off the winter blues.

Sustaining foods such as oats and barley are both highly nutritious and easily digested. Oats are also good for calming a restless mind (see p. 134). Eaten in soups and broths, oats and barley can help relieve stress and fatigue.

### arabic cardamom coffee

A delicious Middle Eastern coffee that peps you up when you need some instant energy. It makes a perfect choice for coffee drinkers since cardamoms not only provide energy but also protect against the potentially harmful effects of caffeine. The ginger adds vitality.

*4 split cardamom pods*
*4 heaped teaspoons finely ground coffee*
*2 heaped teaspoons sugar*
*600ml (1 pint) water*
*1 teaspoon ground ginger, to decorate*

Add the cardamoms, coffee and sugar to the water in a saucepan. Bring to the boil then reduce the heat and simmer for 20 minutes. Sprinkle with ginger before serving in small coffee cups.
4 servings

## gladiators' gruel

Roman gladiators ate barley to give them long-lasting reserves of energy and strength. This warming, solid broth will do the same for you. The sweet-tasting parsnips provide energy through their sugar and starch content; combined with nutritious potatoes and barley they make a hearty soup for cold winter days when we tend to feel lethargic. As an easily digested restorative, this broth is good for the elderly and convalescents. Its high fibre benefits those watching their weight, too.

1 tablespoon olive oil
1 medium onion, peeled and sliced
1.5 litres (2½ pints) vegetable or
   chicken stock
50g (2oz) pearl or pot barley
salt and freshly ground pepper
sprigs of parsley, chives and thyme tied
   together in a bunch
225g (8oz) parsnips, peeled and diced
225g (8oz) potatoes, peeled and chopped
small cabbage heart, shredded
chopped parsley or coriander leaves, to garnish

Heat the oil in a large saucepan and cook the onion for 5 minutes. Add the stock, barley, seasoning and herbs and bring to the boil, then reduce the heat and simmer for 45 minutes. Add the diced parsnips and potatoes and cook on a slightly higher heat for about 30 minutes until soft. Add the cabbage to the saucepan for the last 10 minutes. Remove the bunch of herbs and serve garnished with fresh parsley or coriander. 6 servings

## chinese chicken and corn soup

A traditional energy-boosting tonic from the East, this tasty nutritious soup is full of ingredients that are renowned in China for their energy-giving properties. Ginger and onions stimulate the circulation, chicken increases strength and vitality and corn is a nourishing tonic to the whole system.

1.5 litres (2½ pints) chicken stock
330g (11oz) fresh or tinned sweetcorn kernels
2.5cm (1in) piece of fresh root ginger, grated
300g (10oz) shredded cooked chicken
6-8 spring onions, sliced finely
½ teaspoon sesame oil
salt and freshly ground pepper
chopped fresh coriander, to garnish

Heat the stock for a few minutes in a medium saucepan, then add the sweetcorn, ginger and chicken. Bring to the boil, then reduce the heat and simmer for 5 minutes. Add the spring onions and sesame oil, and season to taste. Cook for a few minutes, then serve garnished with coriander. 6 servings

## ginger cordial

The alliance of ginger and apricots in this recipe is unusual but definitely rewards the adventurous. Not only is this cordial really luscious, it is also great for improving your energy and vitality. Ginger's pungent and warming properties enhance the "fire" in the body, stimulating digestion and circulation, while the apricots, with their abundance of easily digested nutrients and natural sugars, provide the raw materials.

225g (8oz) dried apricots
1 teaspoon ground ginger
½ teaspoon ground cinnamon
¼ teaspoon ground nutmeg
½ teaspoon allspice
4 cloves
600ml (1 pint) ginger ale
½ teaspoon lemon juice

Stew the apricots with the spices in enough water to cover, until soft. Blend until smooth. Add the ginger ale and reheat. Add lemon juice to taste and serve. 4 servings

## italian tomato and thyme soup

A tasty tangy soup that looks as vibrant as it makes you feel! The nutritious tomatoes are rich in antioxidant vitamins A, C and E as well as folic acid and iron. They act to boost energy and vitality, at the same time detoxifying the system. The onions and garlic stimulate the circulation and impart vigour, while the addition of thyme is perfect as it makes a wonderful revitalizing tonic.

*1 tablespoon olive oil*
*1 medium onion, peeled and sliced*
*2 garlic cloves, peeled and chopped finely*
*675g (1½lb) ripe tomatoes, skinned and*
*    chopped*
*300ml (½ pint) water*
*1 tablespoon tomato purée*
*1 tablespoon chopped fresh thyme*
*    or 1-2 teaspoons dried thyme*
*1 teaspoon brown sugar (optional)*
*salt and freshly ground pepper*
*fromage frais or natural yogurt, to garnish*
*a little fresh thyme, to garnish*

Heat the olive oil in a large pan and cook the onion and garlic over a low heat for 5 minutes. Add the remaining ingredients and bring to the boil. Simmer over a low heat, covered, for 20 minutes. Remove from the heat and work through a food mill or fine strainer. Return to the pan, heat and adjust the seasoning if necessary. Garnish with fromage frais or yogurt and thyme. This is delicious served hot or cold. 4 servings

## west indian date and banana energizer

A thick, smooth and deliciously sweet drink for instant and yet long-lasting energy. The warming and energizing spices contrast perfectly with the more cooling and grounding dates and bananas to bring a perfect medley of Caribbean flavours. With their high natural sugar content, bananas and dates are excellent foods for when you are burning a lot of energy. They give extra vitality and endurance and are rich in minerals such as calcium and magnesium to strengthen the nervous system.

*300ml (½ pint) milk (rice, almond, oat, soya,*
*    cow's or goat's)*
*2 ripe bananas*
*8 dried dates (stones removed)*
*a pinch of ground cinnamon and*
*    a pinch of ground cloves, to garnish*

Combine the milk, bananas and dates together in a blender and blend until smooth and creamy. Sprinkle with cinnamon and cloves before drinking. 1 serving

# healthy hair

How good your hair looks reflects your general state of health. If you are feeling off colour or run down, your hair can quickly become dull and lifeless. In today's world, a stressful lifestyle and inadequate diet are the key factors that make hair lose its condition and shine. Nourishing drinks full of nettles, watercress or parsley are abundant in vitamins A and B, and minerals such as calcium, iron, iodine, zinc and silica. These provide the perfect nutrition for a shining head of hair.

## watercress soup

*An ideal dish to nourish and condition your hair, this vibrant green soup not only tastes wonderful but also contains a bevy of nutrients that are vital for healthy hair. By stimulating your appetite, digestion and absorption, watercress nourishes and cleanses at the same time, producing a glow of allround health and vitality.*

1 tablespoon olive oil
3 medium potatoes, peeled and
  cubed
2 garlic cloves, crushed
2 onions, peeled and sliced
2 bunches of watercress, washed
  and chopped
1.5 litres (2½ pints) water
125ml (4fl oz) single cream or milk
125ml (4fl oz) white wine (optional)
2 tablespoons finely chopped fresh
  parsley, chervil or marjoram
salt and freshly ground pepper
single cream and sprigs of
  watercress, to garnish

Heat the oil in a large saucepan. Sauté the potatoes, garlic, onions and watercress for 5 minutes. Add the water, bring to the boil and simmer for about 30 minutes or until the potatoes are soft. Remove from the heat and blend. Stir in the cream or milk, wine, herbs and seasoning. Garnish with a little cream and sprigs of watercress when serving. 6 servings

## nettle beer

*A traditional country drink to have you looking and feeling your best, nettle beer is full of vitamins A and C, calcium, iron, silica and potassium – all of which promote healthy, shining hair – and is only mildly alcoholic. Nettles can help to stimulate hair growth, cleanse the body of toxins and generally improve health.*

450g (1lb) nettle tips
finely peeled rind and juice of
  1 lemon
2.25 litres (4 pints) water
225g (8oz) demerara sugar
15g (½oz) cream of tartar
7.5g (¼oz) dried brewer's yeast
ice cubes
4 lemon slices and 4 young mint
  sprigs, to garnish

Place the nettle tips, lemon rind and water in a large saucepan. Bring to the boil, reduce the heat and simmer for 30 minutes. Strain onto the sugar and cream of tartar in a fermentation bucket and stir well. Start the yeast following the instructions on the packet, then add it to the cooled must in the bucket with the lemon juice. Cover and leave in a warm room for 3 days. Strain the nettle beer into strong bottles (do not screw them up tightly as the beer is slightly effervescent) and leave for a week to settle before drinking. Serve the beer in glasses with ice. Garnish with lemon and mint. 4 servings

## mediterranean make-over

*A sun-filled fruit cup to brighten up your hair, this spicy tango of ingredients is guaranteed to make your tongue tingle as well as your hair sparkle. A beautiful shrub, which grows wild all around the Mediterranean coastline, rosemary stimulates blood circulation to the head, bringing extra nutrients to the hair. Its beneficial properties protect against harmful stress and rejuvenate the whole body.*

*150ml (¼ pint) boiling water*
*1 handful soft tips of rosemary*
   *(with flowers if available)*
*1 tablespoon honey*
*ice cubes*
*600ml (1 pint) orange juice*
*600ml (1 pint) ginger ale*
*sprigs of fresh rosemary, to garnish*

Pour the boiling water over the rosemary in a teapot or heatproof jug. Cover and leave to infuse for 5-10 minutes. Strain through a sieve and stir in the honey. Leave to cool. Place the ice cubes in a large jug. Pour over the rosemary syrup, orange juice and ginger ale. Garnish with sprigs of fresh rosemary. 4 servings

# stimulating the immune system

When the natural defences of our bodies break down we are at risk of developing infections such as bronchitis and pneumonia, viruses such as herpes and flu, autoimmune diseases such as arthritis and multiple sclerosis, and of course cancer.

A healthy lifestyle is the key to an efficient immune system, with plenty of nutritious natural food, a balance of activity and relaxation, and a minimum of pollution and stress which both impose great strain on immunity. In the fight against infection, autoimmune disease and cancer, it is fruits and vegetables that hold the most vital key. Not only do they contain fibre, vitamins and minerals, but also biologically active substances known as phytochemicals.

To produce white blood cells and antibodies, we need to eat enough protein, essential fatty acids, antioxidant vitamins A, B, C and E, and minerals including copper, iron, magnesium, selenium and zinc. A deficiency of just one of these nutrients can have devastating effects on our immunity. Eat brazil nuts, for example, as well as other nuts and seeds and fish for the antioxidant mineral selenium. Dark green vegetables, red fruits such as blackcurrants, raspberries and cherries, eggs and whole grains will provide the iron you need. Members of the brassica family such as broccoli, cabbage and kale stimulate the immune system and the production of antibodies.

## trinidadian spinach soup

The West Indian combination of the sharp taste of spinach and the sweetness of coconut milk is really delicious. In Trinidad they usually eat a version of this soup made with crab meat and known as Callaloo on Sundays after church. Spinach, onions and garlic are all rich in substances to enhance immunity and fight off infection. The antioxidants beta-carotene and vitamin C, and the iron in spinach aid the fight against infection, while the bioflavonoids are thought to help to deactivate carcinogens and help to prevent cancer.

*1 tablespoon olive oil*
*1 onion, peeled and chopped*
*2 garlic cloves, peeled*
*225g (8oz) okra, washed*
*2 medium potatoes, peeled and diced*
*450g (1lb) spinach, washed*
*1 litre (1¾ pints) water or vegetable stock*
*250ml (8fl oz) coconut milk*
*salt and freshly ground pepper*
*freshly grated nutmeg to taste*

Heat the oil in a large pan, add the onion, garlic, okra and potato. Cook gently for 5 minutes. Add the spinach, cover and cook for a further 5 minutes. Add the stock or water, bring to the boil and simmer for 15 minutes or until the vegetables are cooked. Liquidize, then add the coconut milk and seasoning. Reheat and serve garnished with grated nutmeg.
4 servings

## malaysian ginger and lemon tea

An exotic tea to bring a hint of the tropical Far East to your lips. The volatile oils in ginger that give its wonderful pungent taste are highly antiseptic, activating immunity and dispelling bacterial and viral infections, such as colds, tonsillitis, bronchitis and enteritis. The high vitamin C content of lemons helps fight off infection and may ward off cancer. The cleansing properties of both lemons and ginger support the immune system by aiding the elimination of toxins.

*25g (1oz) fresh root ginger, peeled and sliced*
*600ml (1 pint) water*
*squeeze of lemon juice*
*honey to taste*

Place the root ginger in a pan with the water. Bring to the boil, cover and simmer for 20 minutes. Add the lemon juice and sweeten with honey to taste. Drink hot. 2-3 **servings**

## greek skorthalia

One of the most superb and memorable of Greek sauces, reminiscent of lunches in the mountains of Corfu dipping bread and vegetables and watching the sun twinkling on the Aegean. Veritably the best food for the immune system, garlic contains substances that ward off a host of infections, viral, bacterial or fungal, and may block the development of cancers of almost every type, including breast and colon.

*2 medium potatoes, peeled*
*4 large garlic cloves, peeled*
*juice of 1 lemon*
*150ml (¼ pint) water*
*150ml (¼ pint) olive oil*
*6 black peppercorns*
*salt to taste*

Cook the potatoes in water until soft. Drain. Blend all the ingredients together. Delicious stirred into soups and casseroles or as a dip with bread, crackers or raw vegetables. 4 servings

## american fruit defence

Freshly pressed fruit juices are very popular and available in juice bars all over North and South America, especially in hotter areas as they are wonderfully refreshing. Pink grapefruits are high in antioxidant vitamin C, which boosts immunity, and bioflavonoids, which are thought to help to neutralize cancer-causing substances. The bioflavonoids, phenols and tannins in apples and cranberries protect against free radical damage and particularly against viral infections such as colds and herpes.

*100ml (3½fl oz) pink grapefruit juice*
*100ml (3½fl oz) cranberry juice*
*100ml (3½fl oz) apple juice*
*fresh mint or lemon balm leaves, to garnish*

Blend the fruit juices together and garnish with mint or lemon balm leaves. 1 serving

## middle eastern relish

Tomatoes, cucumber and onions, some of the favourite vegetables in Middle Eastern cuisine, are blended together here with garlic and chilli to make a hot spicy vegetable drink to awaken your taste buds and stimulate your defences. Cucumber and tomatoes help to cleanse the body of toxins while the antioxidant vitamins A, C and E, iron, folic acid and bioflavonoids in tomatoes all enhance immunity, and are believed to be helpful in the fight against cancer.

*2 fresh ripe tomatoes, chopped*
*½ medium cucumber, peeled and diced*
*2 spring onions, chopped*
*1 garlic clove*
*100ml (3½fl oz) tomato juice*
*a pinch of chilli powder*
*salt to taste*
*ice cubes (optional)*
*1-2 teaspoons chopped fresh dill, to garnish*

Place all the ingredients except the ice and dill in a liquidizer and blend. Pour over ice in hot weather and garnish with fresh dill. 1 serving

## chinese cinnamon and ginseng preventative

Sweet, aromatic and spicy, this is one of the more appetizing of Chinese herbal decoctions. The essential oil in cinnamon is one of the strongest natural antiseptics known. Its antibacterial, antifungal and antiviral properties guard against a host of infections of the urinary, respiratory and digestive tracts. Ginseng improves our resistence to stress, whether mental or physical, increases white blood cell action and enhances immunity. It is best as a preventative and not for use in acute infections.

*15g (½oz) cinnamon bark*
*1cm (½in) piece of ginseng root*
*600ml (1 pint) water*

Place all the ingredients in a pan. Bring to the boil and simmer, covered, on a low heat for 20 minutes. Strain and drink a cupful twice daily.
2-3 servings

## greek thyme tea

Even the distinctive aroma of wild thyme as it wafts on the warm air in the Greek mountains is enough to enhance your defences against disease. The volatile oils that give thyme its wonderful taste and smell are highly antiseptic, warding off all kinds of infections, and have antioxidant properties, which may help to protect against degenerative disease and cancer. Try sage instead of thyme, if you like, but avoid both thyme and sage if pregnant.

*4 teaspoons fresh or 2 teaspoons dried*
*  thyme leaves*
*600ml (1 pint) boiling water*
*honey to taste (optional)*

Place the thyme in a teapot. Pour on boiling water, cover and leave to infuse for 10-15 minutes. Sweeten with honey if you like. Drink a cupful as a preventative 2-3 times a day.
2-3 servings

# boosting the brain

When our minds are alert we feel alive, we feel good. To achieve this we need to eat well, take regular exercise and allow time to relax and recharge our batteries. Foods affect the chemistry of the brain, and eating the right foods at the right time of the day can really make a difference to the amount of mental energy we have.

Foods containing omega-3 fatty acids such as fish, nuts and tofu, all enhance brain function, and are most suitable for a midday meal. Folic acid in avocado, fresh fruit and green leafy vegetables is a brain food, vital for the conversion of amino acids into the brain chemical serotonin, which affects mood. Acetylcholine, a neurotransmitter for good brain function, is made from vitamin $B_5$ (from green vegetables, brewer's yeast and mushrooms) and choline (from lecithin, nuts, citrus fruits, wheatgerm, beans and pulses).

The brain relies heavily on glucose. Refined sugar provides quick energy but no nutrients. Sugars from foods such as fruit and vegetables provide energy as well as valuable vitamins, minerals and fibre. The glucose is slowly absorbed from them, helping to maintain a constant flow of energy rather than peaks and troughs.

Many of us rely on stimulants, particularly tea and coffee, to get us going in the mornings and keep our brains working through the day. These give us quick bursts of energy followed by a crash, encouraging us to reach for the next caffeine fix. An occasional cup, if you are not a regular caffeine user, can be wonderfully stimulating when you need a flood of mental energy. Regular use will lead to chronic fatigue, poor concentration, anxiety, and often insomnia. Combat the loss of brain power caused by anxiety and stress with drinks containing nerve tonics such as oats, almonds and ginseng that increase our resilience.

## indian morning chai

To kick start your brain in the morning try this stimulating medley of spices which not only exhilarates the taste buds but also invigorates the mind. The warming nature of ginger, black pepper and cinnamon enhances the circulation and sends more blood to the brain, so that you feel awake and alert. The black tea adds its own flavour and is optional. The over-stimulating effect of the caffeine is balanced by the cardamom.

*4 cardamom pods*
*2 sticks cinnamon*
*4 black peppercorns*
*2 teaspoons freshly grated root ginger*
*600ml (1 pint) water*
*1-2 tea bags, Earl Grey or Darjeeling (optional)*
*50ml (2fl oz) soya milk*
*honey to taste*

Place the spices in a pan with the water. Cover and heat gently, without boiling, for 20 minutes. Remove from the heat. Infuse the tea bag(s) for 5 minutes and remove. Add the milk and honey and drink hot. 2-3 servings

## moroccan mint tea

One sip of this traditional Moroccan tea instantly conjures up the labyrinthine streets and alleys of Fez and Marrakesh, donkeys and exotic spices, souks and bazaars, where the summer heat and lethargy are instantly dispelled by this sweet, aromatic and exquisitely refreshing drink. Well known by the Arabs as a brain tonic, mint stimulates blood flow to the head, clearing the mind, enhancing memory and concentration, and invoking creativity and inspiration.

*50-75g (2-3oz) fresh mint leaves (preferably spearmint or peppermint)*
*1-2 tablespoons sugar (traditional but optional)*
*1 litre (1¾ pints) boiling water*

Place the mint (and sugar if used) in a teapot. Pour over the boiling water and leave to steep for 5 minutes. Strain and serve in cups or glasses, each containing a sprig of mint. 4 servings

## almond milk

Sweet and smooth, enlivened by a hint of spice, almond milk is an ideal brain food. Rich in potassium phosphate, calcium and magnesium, all vital nutrients for the central nervous system, almonds improve mental stamina, enhance memory and concentration, and increase resilience to stress. The lecithin acts as an emulsifier and provides choline, which is particularly good for improving the memory. Almond milk makes an ideal substitute for cow's or goat's milk.

*100g (4oz) blanched almonds*
*600ml (1 pint) water*
*2 teaspoons lecithin granules.*
*honey to taste (optional)*
*a pinch of ground cinnamon*

Put the almonds and water in a liquidizer and blend. Add the lecithin granules and blend again. Sweeten with honey if required and serve sprinkled with cinnamon. 2 servings

## old english oatmeal caudle

This stout bevvy was traditionally made with beer and served in English pubs. It was considered a good hot drink for a cold night and was particularly popular with labourers to give them strength for the long drive home after market day. Rich in vitamins and minerals, oats increase both physical and mental energy, and are in fact one of the best tonics for the nervous system. The added wheatgerm provides vital choline.

*1 handful fine oatmeal*
*2 teaspoons wheatgerm*
*300ml (½ pint) ginger ale*
*300ml (½ pint) water*
*6 cloves*
*a pinch of ground nutmeg*
*2.5cm (1in) piece of root ginger, peeled and*
  *sliced or grated*
*honey to taste*
*a few pieces of lemon peel, to garnish*

Place all the ingredients except the honey and lemon peel in a pan and boil for 30 minutes, stirring frequently. If the mixture becomes too thick, add a little more water or ginger ale. Sweeten with honey to taste and serve sprinkled with lemon peel. 2-3 servings

## ginseng and cardamom brain tonic

Sweet and aromatic, this flavoursome decoction cannot be recommended highly enough to those who want to improve their mental performance. In India cardamom is recognized as one of the best stimulants to the mind, enhancing clarity and concentration. Ginseng has been shown through extensive research to improve memory and overall mental capacity, and is particularly useful for protecting against the effects of aging on the function of the brain.

*25g (1oz) whole dried ginseng root*
*2 litres (3½ pints) water*
*15g (½oz) cardamon pods*

Place the ginseng in a pan with the water. Bring to the boil and simmer on a low heat for 30 minutes until the liquid is reduced by half. Add the cardamom, cover and heat gently, without boiling, for a further 20 minutes. Strain. Drink a cupful each morning. Store in the refrigerator and reheat when required. 8 servings

## cold awakening

When nothing other than a cup of real coffee will do to enable you to finish that job you have been putting off for weeks, try this spicy version of iced coffee. It is particularly refreshing on a hot summer's day after a good lunch when lethargy might be threatening, albeit rather pleasantly, to take over the brain. The Middle Eastern tradition of combining cardamom with coffee works a treat and tastes delicious.

*1 tablespoon freshly ground coffee*
*1 teaspoon ground nutmeg*
*1 teaspoon ground cardamom*
*600ml (1 pint) boiling water*
*2 tablespoons vanilla ice cream*
*1 tablespoon honey*
*ice cubes*
*a little ground cardamom, to garnish*

Place the coffee, nutmeg and cardamom in a pot and pour on boiling water. Leave to stand until cold. Strain into a bowl or liquidizer and blend with the ice cream and honey. Pour into glasses over ice cubes and sprinkle with ground cardamom. 2-3 servings

drinks for recovering from illness

# drinks for recovering from illness

It may seem extraordinary and perhaps to some unbelievable, but the fact is that the everyday foodstuffs that can be found in most people's kitchens or grown in their vegetable and herb gardens provide us with potent medicines to prevent and to treat almost every ill. This is nothing new, for our ancestors depended entirely upon such things and treated them with the respect they deserve for thousands of years. It is only in the last century that modern drugs have superseded the more gentle and apparently old-fashioned medicines from our vegetable racks and fruit bowls and caused us largely to forget their amazing medicinal value.

Scientists worldwide are still pursuing their search for new cures for age-old ills, such as heart disease, circulatory problems, infections, immune problems and cancer, and the world of plants is a primary focus. In their exciting discoveries they are identifying chemically active substances within familiar foods such as cabbage, carrots, beans, apples and cherries which help us to understand our forebears' use of such foods as medicines for particular ills and to reinstate these miraculous healers to the place in our lives that they deserve. So-called folk remedies such as cabbage juice for arthritis, leeks for a sore throat, onions for the heart, garlic for infections and carrots to improve eyesight have been found to have merit in our modern world after all.

There are several ways in which edible plants can benefit our health directly. They provide our bodies with a range of vital nutrients that are the building blocks for making new cells, repairing damage and fighting off disease. Their cellulose provides fibre which, because it is not broken down in the bowel, helps to maintain a healthy gut. In addition they contain a variety of pharmacologically active constituents, including mucilage, volatile oils, antioxidants and phytosterols, which have specifically therapeutic effects. Tomatoes, carrots, parsley and dandelion leaves, to illustrate, are rich in antioxidants beta-carotene and vitamin C which may help to delay the aging process, enhance immunity, and prevent heart and arterial disease as well as some cancers. Citrus fruits, berries, broccoli, cherries, papaya, grapes and melon are all rich in bioflavonoids which also act as antioxidants. In addition their antimicrobial properties help us to fight off a whole range of infections. They also have a synergistic relationship with vitamin C and have the ability to bind with toxic metals and carry them out of the body.

The more we broaden our knowledge of the amazing therapeutic properties of foods, the more able we will be to utilize them to our advantage. Our food and drinks can be our medicines and this is clearly to be seen in the following pages where you can find recipes that not only taste mouth-wateringly good but also address a wide range of common ailments. Let's drink to your health and your recovery.

# clearing coughs

Coughing is nature's way of clearing the airways. It is a reflex response to any substance that threatens to block the throat or bronchial tubes – food particles, irritants from the atmosphere, or irritation and phlegm from an infection.

A healthy immune system is the key to warding off colds and coughs, particularly in the winter when infections are rife. A good diet with regular exercise, rest and relaxation will help to keep infections at bay. Take plenty of your exercise outdoors to keep your lungs healthy, and try to minimize the hours spent in stuffy overheated rooms.

To maximize your resistance to the infections that cause coughs there is a wealth of remedies from the plant kingdom to help you. The best are vitamin C-rich foods, such as citrus fruits, sweet peppers, black-currants, blackberries, apples and green vegetables. They stimulate the little hairs lining the bronchi in the lungs and help them to clear out toxins and irritants efficiently.

Onions, leeks and garlic have antiseptic qualities and can prevent and clear infection from the chest. Turnips and brassicas, such as cabbage, stimulate the immune system and also fight infection. Carrots have an expectorant action that can clear phlegm from the throat, while spices such as ginger and cayenne can decongest the airways.

## caribbean cordial

This fiery combination of ginger and lemon, a popular healing drink in the West Indies, warms and stimulates the respiratory tract, clearing phlegm and relieving coughs and congestion. Rich in vitamin C, this cordial boosts immunity to infection.

*50g (2oz) root ginger, bruised*
*1 lemon, thinly sliced*
*1.5 litres (2½ pints) water*
*900g (2lb) brown sugar*
*still or sparkling mineral water to dilute*

Put the root ginger and lemon in water in a covered saucepan. Bring to the boil then simmer for 45 minutes. Remove from the heat, add the sugar and stir until dissolved. Strain into a bottle, seal and store. To drink, dilute approximately ⅓ cordial to ⅔ water.

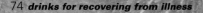

## thyme syrup

This sweet fragrant syrup from Greece makes an excellent remedy for all kinds of coughs. Thyme is highly antiseptic and, with its expectorant action, chases away infection and clears congestion from the chest. A perfect syrup for children with its smooth, velvety texture and delicious taste.

*50g (2oz) fresh or 25g (1oz) dried thyme leaves*
*600ml (1 pint) boiling water*
*300g (10oz) runny honey*
*300g (10oz) sugar*

Place the thyme in a teapot. Pour on boiling water, cover and leave to infuse for 10-15 minutes. Heat the infusion with the honey and sugar in a stainless steel or enamel saucepan. Stir the mixture as it starts to thicken and skim off any scum from the surface. Leave to cool. Pour into a cork-stoppered bottle and store in the refrigerator. Take 2 teaspoons, 3 times daily for chronic problems, and every 2 hours for acute conditions in children.

## cabbage and carrot juice

This nourishing vegetable juice makes an excellent alternative to a light meal for when your body is fighting infection and you do not want to overburden the digestive tract with heavy food. Cabbage and carrots stimulate the immune system and the production of antibodies and make good remedies for fighting off bacterial and viral infections. Their antimicrobial properties have an affinity for the respiratory system where they also have an expectorant action. The addition of celery makes this recipe more tasty and provides extra vitamins and minerals to support the immune system.

*250ml (8fl oz) cabbage juice*
*125ml (4fl oz) carrot juice*
*125ml (4fl oz) celery juice*
*chopped fresh coriander leaves, to garnish*

Blend the vegetable juices together and serve with a garnish of coriander. Drink a cupful 3 times daily. 2 servings

# sore throats

At the first sign of a sore throat your instinct is probably to reach for an antiseptic gargle and prepare for the onslaught of the cold or flu to come. The right drinks support our immune system and at the same time soothe away some of the rawness and discomfort in the throat. You shouldn't be without echinacea tincture at such times. Drink ¼ teaspoonful in a little bit of water every two hours.

So that every effort can be reserved for throwing off the infection it is best not to overburden your body with heavy food to digest and absorb. Fruity drinks bursting with vitamin C and bioflavonoids or vegetable juices packed with vitamins and minerals can replace full meals. Raspberries, cherries, oranges and lemons, blackcurrants and blueberries, celery, beetroot, carrots and cabbage provide a great selection to choose from. Soups with plenty of onions, garlic and leeks are ideal for soothing sore throats and combating infection.

The world of herbs offers many remedies with antimicrobial properties to help fight off both viral and bacterial infections. Infusions of sage, thyme, mint and chamomile can be made into tasty cocktails. Spices, such as ginger and cinnamon, are highly antiseptic, and taste great. By stimulating the circulation and increasing vital energy they aid elimination of toxins and strengthen the battle against infection.

## raspberry and cider vinegar

This old English recipe with its happy alliance of sweet and sour tastes, is a traditional remedy for soothing sore throats. Raspberries are crammed with vitamins and minerals for the immune system. Their antiseptic and astringent effects ease soreness and protect the mucous membranes of the throat against infection. The acidity of the cider vinegar inhibits micro-organisms and, when sipped frequently, cools heat and inflammation.

*1kg (2¼lb) fresh raspberries, washed*
*600ml (1 pint) cider vinegar*

Place the raspberries in a large jar and cover with the cider vinegar. Leave to macerate in a cool dark place for two weeks. Strain through a nylon sieve and discard the raspberry pulp. Store the vinegar in a clean bottle. Dilute 1 teaspoon in a cup of water, or to taste, and drink 3 times a day. This mixture can also be used as a gargle.

## greek sage and thyme infusion

This aromatic tisane is quick and easy to make and ideal for relieving sore throats At the first signs of discomfort, sip a cupful every 2 hours or so. Both sage and thyme grow wild on Greek hillsides, and the essential oils that lend them their distinctive flavour have powerful antiseptic properties and an affinity for the respiratory tract. They are excellent remedies for the colds, coughs, fevers and flu that might accompany or proceed from a sore throat. Avoid thyme and sage if pregnant.

*15g (½oz) dried or 30g (1oz) fresh thyme*
*15g (½oz) dried or 30g (1oz) fresh sage*
*600ml (1 pint) boiling water*

Place the herbs in a large teapot and pour over boiling water. Cover and leave to infuse for 10-15 minutes. Drink hot. 2-3 servings

## spiced lemonade

The familiar combination of honey, lemon and spices tastes exquisite and provides a time-tested remedy for soothing sore throats and banishing respiratory infections. The warming spices, with their antimicrobial essential oils and decongestant properties, are perfect for fighting colds and flu. Lemon juice, like honey, is a great antiseptic and is high in vitamin C, providing a boost to the immune system. Honey is wonderfully soothing to the throat.

*1.2 litres (2 pints) water*
*100g (4oz) sugar*
*4 cloves*
*½ teaspoon ground allspice*
*1 cinnamon stick*
*juice of 4 lemons*
*3-6cm (1-2in) strips of lemon peel, to garnish*

Put the water into a preserving pan with the sugar and spices. Bring slowly to the boil, cover and simmer for 10 minutes. Strain then stir in the lemon juice. Drink hot with a twist of lemon.
4 servings

## flu-busters

When seeing off winter colds and flu, start treating yourself smartly at the first sign of achy limbs, a sore throat, a runny nose or sneezing. The aim is to cleanse the system of toxins, which may have lowered vitality and added to infection in the first place, and to enhance the efforts of the immune system in its fight against infection.

### beet borscht cocktail

*A favourite Eastern European classic, used down the ages for vital sustenance during long, hard winters. Beetroot has a long-held reputation for stimulating immunity, reducing fevers, and enhancing the elimination of toxins by stimulating liver, bowel and kidney function. It also stimulates the lymphatic system, aiding immunity, and helps to clear irritating catarrh and respiratory congestion. Carrots promote bowel activity and cucumber aids the elimination of toxins through the kidneys.*

*125ml (4fl oz) beetroot juice*
*125ml (4fl oz) carrot juice*
*90ml (3fl oz) cucumber juice*
*1 tablespoon lemon juice*
*1 tablespoon natural live yogurt*

Blend all the juices together and serve topped with a dollop of yogurt. Drink a glassful twice daily while acute symptoms last. 1 serving

### old english elderflower and peppermint tea

*A traditional old country recipe using a refreshing, decongestant combination of ingredients. Peppermint helps to clear the airways and increases the circulation, promoting sweating, thereby reducing fevers. Its refreshing-tasting volatile oils have an antimicrobial action, enhancing the efforts of the immune system. Elderflowers similarly help to clear catarrh, reduce fevers, enhance immunity and cleanse the system of toxins.*

*1 teaspoon dried or 2 teaspoons*
 *fresh elderflowers*
*1 teaspoon dried or 2 teaspoons*
 *fresh peppermint leaves*
*600ml (1 pint) boiling water*
 *honey to taste (optional)*

Place the herbs in a teapot and pour over boiling water. Cover and leave to infuse for 10 minutes. Drink a cupful every 2 hours if symptoms are acute. Sweeten with honey if you like.

2-3 servings

## kashmir spicy tea

*According to ancient Ayurvedic principles, ginger is the most sattvic of all the spices, inducing a calm, meditative state of mind. This old Indian drink is a decoction of spices that increase circulation, help throw off fevers and aid the body's fight against infection. It is also a great decongestant for a stuffed-up nose or a congested chest.*

*15g (½oz) fresh root ginger, sliced*
*1 stick cinnamon*
*4 cloves*
*4 black peppercorns*
*1 teaspoon coriander seeds*
*600ml (1 pint) cold water*
*honey to taste (optional)*
*lemon slices (optional)*

Put the spices and water in a pan and bring to the boil. Cover and simmer for 10-15 minutes, then strain. Sweeten with honey or add a slice of lemon. Drink a cupful, as hot as possible, 3 to 6 times daily while acute symptoms last. 2-3 servings

# catarrhal congestion

A blocked nose, an irritating throat and a congested chest can make you feel lousy and bring on catarrh from mucus-secreting cells which produce more liquid to dilute irritants and eliminate them from the body. Greek sage and thyme infusion (see p. 77) taken every two hours is ideal for chasing away such irritating infections as colds and flu.

Chronic catarrh due to excess toxins in your system may be relieved by cleansing drinks, such as fennel tea, carrot and celery juices or nettle and cabbage soup, (see p. 133). When atmospheric pollution, smoke, paint or central heating contribute to catarrh, try soothing decoctions of licorice, marshmallow or mullein. Catarrh could be caused by an allergy such as hay fever or allergic rhinitis, related to a sensitivity to animal dander, grass pollen, milk or wheat products. Drinks made with nettles, chamomile, lemon balm, yarrow and coriander help reduce such sensitivity.

Cut out mucus-forming foods from your diet, especially milk products, wheat and sugar, and drink decongestant juices made with fruit such as cherries, blackcurrants, strawberries, plums, apples and mangoes, and vegetables such as carrots, beetroot, spinach and celery. Pungent foods and herbs such as garlic, onion, leeks, ginger, thyme, cinnamon and mint stimulate the respiratory system and help to move and liquify catarrh. They are also expectorants, helping to clear mucus from your chest.

## middle eastern melody

The delightfully aromatic coriander leaves make the sweet blend of carrot and orange juice just sing on your tongue. Carrots have a wonderful ability to soothe the mucous membranes throughout the body, helping to reduce irritation. Their cleansing properties and expec- torant action are ideal for decongesting the airways. Fresh coriander, like orange juice, is rich in vitamins A and C and has been used for centuries in the East for relieving catarrh and allergic rhinitis.

*125ml (4fl oz) carrot juice*
*125ml (4fl oz) orange juice*
*4 tablespoons finely chopped coriander leaves*
*ice cubes*
*fresh coriander sprigs, to garnish*

Mix together the juices and chopped coriander. Pour into a glass half filled with ice and serve garnished with coriander sprigs. 1 serving

## nero's nectar

The Roman emperor, Nero, was extremely fond of onions and leeks to treat his colds and sore throats. The unusual combination of onion and honey may not titillate everybody's taste buds but the courageous will be rewarded. Raw onions are powerfully antiseptic and their pungency stimulates the respiratory system, breaking up mucous congestion in the nose and chest. Honey with its antiseptic and expectorant properties is an ideal therapeutic partner.

*2 medium onions, peeled and chopped*
*2 tablespoons honey*

Place the onions in a bowl, drizzle with the honey and leave, covered, at room temperature overnight to produce a juice. Take a teaspoonful every 2 hours while symptoms last.

## african mango smoothie

In the Ivory Coast in the mango season they make a luscious dessert to use up a glut of ripe mangoes which doubles as a luxuriously thick drink to clear catarrhal congestion. Mangoes act as a wonderful decongestant in the respiratory system and their action is enhanced by the cleansing and astringent effect of limes. Rice milk blends very well with the fruit and contributes a soothing action throughout the respiratory tract.

*2 ripe mangoes*
*juice of ½ lime*
*300ml (½ pint) rice milk*
*fresh mint sprigs, to garnish*

Extract all the mango flesh and place in a blender with the lime juice and rice milk. Blend until smooth and serve decorated with fresh mint leaves. 1-2 servings

## onion wine

Perhaps a more attractive way to take onion is this wine with warming and decongestant effects. The pungency of the onion blends well with the slight tang of white wine. Honey not only augments the effectiveness of this drink in clearing the airways but also provides that "spoonful of sugar to help the medicine go down".

*300g (10oz) onion, finely chopped*
*4 tablespoons honey*
*600ml (1 pint) white wine*

Add the onion and honey to the wine in a large jar with a lid. Leave to infuse for 48 hours, shaking frequently. Strain. Take a tablespoonful 3-6 times daily, depending on the severity of the congestion. Stored in the refrigerator, this wine will keep for up to 3 days.

# headaches and migraines

Everybody has the occasional headache, perhaps with a cold or fever or after a tense and tiring day. Some people are unlucky enough to get them once a week, normally as a result of tension in the head and neck muscles. Other precipitating factors include eye problems, hangovers, catarrh, sinusitis, allergies and high blood pressure.

A small percentage of headache sufferers get migraine, a much more intense and debilitating type, which can be accompanied often by nausea, vomiting, visual disturbances and sensitivity to light. Migraines are caused by constriction and dilation of the blood vessels going to the head. Migraine sufferers tend to be high achievers and perfectionists, prone to tension and frustration, and may need to find ways of helping themselves to be more relaxed. Women tend to suffer from migraine more than men, especially around their menstrual periods due to changes in oestrogen levels.

If you are prone to headaches or migraine, prevention is always better than cure. There are many factors that can act as triggers. Skipping meals and going on crash diets are not a good idea as they cause hypoglycaemia (low blood sugar), which can precipitate a headache. Caffeinated drinks and high sugar foods also predispose to hypoglycaemia. Certain foods and drinks are known to act as triggers and should be avoided if you suffer from headaches. These include coffee, tea, chocolate, cocoa, cola, yeast extract, oranges, bananas, hard cheeses, alcohol, pork products and cream. Drink plenty of fluids and eat regular meals with an abundance of oily fish, nuts and seeds, whole grains and fresh vegetables.

Before you reach for conventional pain killers to prevent or relieve your headache, try some herbal teas which may well do the trick. Bay leaves, feverfew, ginkgo, rosemary, lemon balm and peppermint are the first herbs that come to mind. All over Asia they use ginger to prevent headaches and migraine, and in Central and South America hot chilli peppers are used, the capsaicin which gives them their pungency, acting as a marvellous pain killer.

## peruvian pain killer

This fiery combination of two of the most popular spices in South America has a powerful bite so is not a remedy for the fainthearted. Coriander seeds with their excellent digestive properties are good for relieving headaches due to digestive disturbances. The chilli, by stimulating the secretion of endorphins from the brain, blocks pain and at the same time induces a wonderful feeling of wellbeing.

*2 teaspoons coriander seeds*
*5 cloves*
*1 teaspoon chilli powder*
*600ml (1 pint) water*
*honey to taste*

Place the spices in a pan with the water and bring to the boil. Cover and leave to simmer for 10 minutes. Sweeten with honey and drink ½ a cupful when required. 4-6 servings

## mediterranean magic

The delightful scent and flavour of this light aromatic tisane brings images of Mediterranean sea and sun to mind and before you know it those tense, tight muscles that bring on stress headaches have relaxed. Basil and lemon balm have wonderful calming effects and provide a perfect antidote to a variety of stress-related symptoms including headaches and migraines.

*1 tablespoon fresh basil leaves*
*1 tablespoon fresh lemon balm leaves*
*600ml (1 pint) boiling water*

Place the herbs in a teapot and pour over boiling water. Cover and leave to infuse for 10-15 minutes. Drink a cupful when required. 2-3 servings

## carrot and rosemary juice

In this recipe the sweet, rather bland-tasting carrot juice is brought to life by the distinctive and rather penetrating flavour of rosemary. With their ability to improve digestion and liver function, and to dilate blood vessels, carrots help to detoxify the system and maintain good circulation to the head. By improving blood flow to the head, relaxing tension and stimulating the function of the liver, rosemary makes one of the best remedies for headaches and migraine.

*125ml (4fl oz) carrot juice*
*125ml (4fl oz) celery juice*
*3 soft sprigs of fresh rosemary*
*freshly ground pepper*

Blend the carrot and celery juices and rosemary together in a blender, season with pepper and drink immediately. Drink a cupful regularly as a preventative.  1 serving

# sinusitis

Sinusitis is an irritating, often painful, condition. Inflammation and infection of the sinuses – the bony cavities surrounding the eyes and nasal passages – develops when they become filled with mucus. Acute sinusitis causes pain and pressure across the nose, cheeks and forehead and sometimes an intense headache. It may develop from catarrhal congestion after a cold or flu, or with hay fever. Chronic sinus congestion is often related to environmental pollution or an excess of body toxins, or is an accompaniment of allergic rhinitis.

To reduce catarrhal congestion make sure that you drink plenty of fluids to flush toxins through the system and to keep your bowels moving. Take regular aerobic exercise in the fresh air and if you work in a stuffy atmosphere keep a window open when you can. It is always best to cut mucus-forming foods out of your diet until the condition clears. These include all milk products, especially fatty cheese and milk, refined cereals especially bread and pasta, and sugar. At the same time there are plenty of ingredients you can use in your food and drinks which actually help to clear catarrh and infection.

Blackcurrants, apples, blueberries, cherries, lemons, grapefruits, mangoes and pineapples all have decongestant properties and boost the body's fight against infection. Similarly vegetables such as leeks, onions, carrots and cabbage, herbs including garlic, borage, elderflower, limeflower, coriander, chamomile, mint, thyme and lemon balm, and warming spices like ginger, cinnamon, caraway and cayenne can be made into soups, juices and herbal teas to clear catarrh and infection in the sinuses. Drinks are best taken hot as the heat itself also helps to move phlegm.

## panamanian indian cure

Apparently the Choco Indians of Panama eat ripe guavas to clear catarrhal congestion and certainly it is hard to envisage a more pleasant way of relieving sinusitis. These sweet succulent fruits make a delightfully exotic juice when combined with mango and grapefruit, which also clear mucus from the body and provide a wealth of nutrients to support the immune system in its fight against infection.

*45ml (1½fl oz) pink grapefruit juice*
*90ml (3fl oz) guava juice*
*90ml (3fl oz) mango juice*
*fresh lemon balm leaves, to garnish*

Combine the fruit juices. If the weather is hot pour into glasses over ice and garnish with lemon balm leaves. 1 serving

## cabbage and coriander syrup

This may not sound like the most enticing of combinations but it is certainly a good remedy for clearing the sinuses. Cabbage is a wonderful detoxifier, hastening the elimination of toxins from the body. It also stimulates the immune system and the production of antibodies and has a disinfectant action with a particular affinity with the respiratory tract. Coriander seeds not only make the taste more interesting but have their own decongestant and antiseptic properties.

*2 teaspoons coriander seeds*
*½ cabbage, chopped finely*
*enough runny honey to cover cabbage*

Crush the coriander seeds using a pestle and mortar. Place the crushed seeds in a large bowl with the cabbage and cover with honey. Leave overnight and then strain the syrup through a sieve. Take 1-2 teaspoons 3 times daily until your sinuses improve.

## old english decongestant

A hot infusion of elderflowers, yarrow and peppermint is a traditional English recipe for relieving the symptoms of colds, flu, fevers, catarrh and sinus congestion. This light aromatic tisane tastes very pleasant and makes a good drink for the winter as it stimulates the circulation, clears phlegm and enhances immunity but equally well makes a delightfully refreshing drink for a hot summer's day.

*1 teaspoon dried or 2 teaspoons fresh*
  *elderflowers*
*1 teaspoon dried or 2 teaspoons fresh*
  *limeflowers*
*1 teaspoon dried or 2 teaspoons fresh*
  *peppermint leaves*
*1 teaspoon dried or 2 teaspoons fresh yarrow*
*600ml (1 pint) boiling water*
*honey to taste*

Place the herbs in a teapot and pour over boiling water. Cover and leave to infuse for 10-15 minutes. Sweeten with honey if you like and drink a cupful, hot, 3-6 times a day until the congestion clears. 2-3 servings

# children's fevers

Fevers produced by childhood illnesses represent a strong and vital response to toxins and provide an opportunity for the child to cleanse the system and throw off toxins accumulated not only during the child's life but also inherited from parents at the embryonic stage of development.

We can aid this process by not giving a child with a fever solid food, just plenty to drink. This encourages sweating and elimination of toxins via the pores as well as through the kidneys and bladder. There are certain herbs which actually encourage sweating which would be ideal here, including basil, lime-flower, lemon balm, elderflower, peppermint, yarrow, chamomile, ginger and cinnamon.

Drinks prepared from fruits, vegetables and herbs packed with vitamins, minerals and trace elements will provide nutritional support for the immune system in its fight against infection. Those with a mild laxative action will also help to speed the cleansing process. Apples, apricots, blackberries, bilberries, blackcurrants, carrots, peas, celery, garlic and onions would all be beneficial.

## english blackberry cordial

*This sweet spicy cordial is delicious enough to be loved by children and provides a great remedy for aiding the body's fight against infection and throwing off a fever at the same time. Blackberries are packed with vitamin C and bioflavonoids, they have a decongestant action and clear toxins from the body through their laxative and diuretic effects. The spices increase sweating by stimulating the circulation and have powerful anti-microbial properties.*

*900g (2lb) ripe blackberries or enough to produce 600ml (1 pint) juice*
*6 tablespoons runny honey*
*10 cloves*
*5 slices fresh root ginger*
*1 teaspoon ground cinnamon*

Press the ripe, raw blackberries through a sieve to obtain the juice. Place in a pan and add the honey and spices. Bring to the boil over a low heat, stirring until the honey has dissolved. Simmer for 5 minutes. Leave to cool. To drink add hot water and dilute to taste. Drink a cupful every 2 hours.

## french limeflower and lemon balm tea

*This light fragrant tea with a hint of lemon, loved by the French, is an excellent cooling remedy for reducing children's fevers. When taken hot both lemon balm and limeflowers have a diaphoretic action, increasing blood supply to the skin and producing sweating. The tea also has a decongestant effect and will speed sore throats, colds, coughs and flu on their way.*

*2 teaspoons fresh or 1 teaspoon dried limeflowers*
*2 teaspoons fresh lemon balm*
*600ml (1pint) water*

Place the herbs in a teapot and pour over boiling water. Cover and leave to infuse for 10 minutes. Sweeten with honey. Drink a cupful of warm tea every two hours. 2-3 servings

## blackcurrant and apple rob

*A lovely refreshing drink with a tangy fruit flavour which your children can enjoy throughout the day when they have a fever. All three fruits in this recipe have antiseptic properties and are rich in vitamin C and bioflavonoids which enhance the body's fight against infection. At the same time they have a decongestant action, helping to relieve the catarrhal congestion accompanying the respiratory infections which often give rise to children's fevers.*

2 apples, cored and chopped
50g (2oz) blackcurrants
450ml (16fl oz) water
2 teaspoons lemon juice
honey to taste

Place the apple and blackcurrants in a pan with the water and bring to the boil. Simmer for 10 minutes then strain. Stir in lemon juice and honey and serve hot.

2 servings

# hangovers

That nauseating headache and that terrible taste in your mouth are the price you pay sometimes for a night's partying or even just a few quiet drinks with a friend. Naturally the best way to avoid a hangover is to drink alcohol only in moderation or not at all. In some circumstances just one or two drinks can leave you feeling groggy the next day. This may be due to the fact that you drank on an empty stomach or that you are particularly susceptible to the effects of alcohol – if you only drink occasionally or if your liver is rather sluggish, you may suffer more than others.

Alcohol acts as a diuretic, increasing the flow of urine, and heats the body causing perspiration. Dehydration resulting from excessive urination and sweating is the major cause of a hangover. The loss of valuable minerals and trace elements through urination also contributes to your headache. This is the reason why people often advise you to drink lots of water before and after your night's revelry. And if you nibble hors d'oeuvres or eat a meal while you drink, you will slow the absorption of the alcohol into your blood stream and give your liver a chance to deal with it properly. Drinking slowly over a period of a few hours will also help in this respect.

Unfortunately, there is no natural hangover cure that guarantees your ability to drink all night and function well the following day. However, there are some ways of minimizing the penalties of drinking moderately. Alcohol affects the absorption and metabolism of nutrients, including vitamins A, B and C, calcium, magnesium and zinc. The vitamins A and C in fresh fruit and vegetable juices will replenish nutrients and help to clear alcohol out of the system quickly, so a glass of grapefruit or apple juice before and after drinking could be just the ticket. The fructose in fruit juice also helps the body to metabolize alcohol faster while the liquid in such drinks flushes toxins out of the system and replaces liquid lost through dehydration.

## sri lankan soother

This sharp, rather exhilarating drink has long been recommended by Ayurvedic doctors for relieving the symptoms of overindulgence. The lime and grapefruit provide plenty of vitamin C and fructose and have a cleansing effect, restoring an overworked liver and aiding its metabolism of toxins. The sweet and spicy cumin aids digestion, supports the liver and enhances our ability to deal with toxins including alcohol.

*600ml (1 pint) grapefruit juice*
*2 teaspoons lime juice*
*1 teaspoon ground cumin*

Blend the ingredients together and drink preferably both before and after drinking alcohol.
2-3 servings

## roman relief

While the taste of cabbage juice may not appeal to everyone, especially when feeling a little fragile the morning after the night before, it is one of the best remedies for a hangover. The distinctive tastes of celery and coriander do a good job at disguising the flavour and help to lessen the intoxicating effects of alcohol. Cabbage was popular with the Romans for preventing drunkenness and as a remedy for headaches and hangovers. We know now that it contains glutamine, a substance which protects the liver against the effects of alcohol.

*250ml (8fl oz) fresh cabbage juice*
*250ml (8fl oz) fresh celery juice*
*2 teaspoons fresh coriander leaves*

Blend the vegetable juices together and stir in the coriander when serving, reserving a few leaves to garnish. 2 servings

## elizabethan rosemary and lemon syrup

A glass or two of this wonderfully aromatic cordial will soon have you back on your feet. Rosemary used to be sold by 17th-century English apothecaries as a cure for a hangover. This is not hard to understand for the bitters in rosemary stimulate the liver and help cleanse the system of toxins. The lemon juice also acts as a tonic to the liver, especially when drunk on an empty stomach, and helps replace vitamin C.

*600ml (1 pint) rosemary sprigs, gently pressed*
*    down in a measuring jug*
*600ml (1 pint) boiling water*
*juice of 1 lemon*
*450g (1lb) sugar*

Place the rosemary in a pot or jug and pour over boiling water. Cover and leave to infuse for 10 minutes. Strain into a pan and add the lemon juice and sugar. Heat slowly, stirring, until the sugar has dissolved. Boil briskly for 5-8 minutes or until the syrup starts to thicken. Remove from the heat and when cool pour into jars or bottles. Seal with airtight lids when cold. Take 1-2 tablespoons as required until your hangover subsides.

# insomnia

A good night's sleep for at least six to eight hours is vital for our general health and to enable us to perform at our best during our waking hours. Insomnia is largely caused by stress and tension, often related to a major upheaval in life, a bereavement, financial worries or depression. Before you rush to the doctor for sleeping pills try some natural treatments and strategies that are not addictive and may actually enhance your health.

Make sure that you eat well and include plenty of foods to nourish the nervous system such as oats, whole grains, fresh fruit and vegetables, nuts and seeds. If you have sleep problems it is always best to avoid stimulants including sugar, sweets, caffeine and smoking, especially near bedtime. Also avoid stimulating the brain at night by working at your desk, catching up on jobs unfinished in the daytime. It is better to get your body programmed for sleep in the evening by doing something that relaxes you.

Don't eat a large meal near bedtime and try to go to bed at the same time each night so that you develop a good sleep pattern. Have a comforting drink such as hot milk and honey, lemon balm, lavender, chamomile or limeflower tea before bed and if you feel peckish a light snack so that if you have had an early evening meal you do not wake up in the night because you are hungry. Remember to take regular exercise as this is a great antidote to stress, which can be a cause of sleeplessness.

## scandanavian soother

No matter where you travel in Scandanavia you will find that exquisitely aromatic herb dill enlivening vegetable dishes, sauces, soups and salads. It is the very substances that impart dill's lovely flavour that give its wonderful relaxant effect on the smooth muscle throughout the body and on the central nervous system. It is perfect in this lettuce soup which has been a famous remedy for nervous tension and insomnia for centuries.

*1 tablespoon olive oil*
*2 medium onions, peeled and sliced*
*2 potatoes, peeled and diced*
*1 garlic clove, crushed*
*1 large lettuce, chopped*
*900ml (1½ pints) vegetable or chicken stock*
*salt and freshly ground pepper*
*3 tablespoons thick natural yogurt*
*2 tablespoons fresh dill, chopped*

Heat the oil in a large pan and gently fry the onions, potatoes and garlic for 5 minutes. Add the lettuce to the pan with the stock and seasoning. Bring to the boil, cover and simmer over a low heat for 20 minutes. Allow to cool a little before blending. Add the yogurt and half of the dill then refrigerate for about 3 hours. Garnish with the remaining dill when serving.
4 servings

## english lettuce tea

The white latex that exudes from the stem of a lettuce when you pick it is known as "lettuce opium" because it resembles in appearance and action that extracted from the opium poppy. The whole vegetable has a sedative effect, helping to calm restlessness and anxiety and induce sleep. Lettuce tea is, in fact, a well-known old English recipe for insomnia. Mint helps to counteract the slight bitterness of the lettuce and make a really quite palatable bedtime drink.

*3-4 large lettuce leaves*
*300ml (½ pint) water*
*2 sprigs fresh mint*

Simmer the lettuce leaves in the water in a covered pan for 15 minutes. Remove from the heat and add the mint. Leave for a further 5 minutes. Strain and drink before retiring.
1 serving

## greek chamomile and limeflower tea

The honey-sweet aroma from the flower-laden lime trees scenting the night air in old Corfu is enough to relax tense muscles and induce a good night's sleep. Put the flowers in a tisane with the equally relaxing chamomile flowers, which grow wild all over the island in summer, and you have a wonderful remedy for insomnia. Drink a cupful before retiring.

*2 teaspoons limeflowers*
*2 teaspoons chamomile flowers*
*600ml (1 pint) boiling water*
*honey to taste*

Place the herbs in a teapot and pour over boiling water. Cover and leave to infuse for 10 minutes. Sweeten with honey if required.
2-3 servings

# arthritis

The inflammation, pain and stiffness in the joints of arthritis – whether rheumatoid arthritis, osteoarthritis or gout – can be crippling. You can take steps yourself to help prevent the onset or alleviate the symptoms of arthritis: be careful about what you eat; correct your posture; take plenty of exercise; take steps to relieve stress and emotional tensions; and keep your weight down.

Certain foods can actually contribute to joint inflammation – particular culprits are tomatoes and other members of the potato family, citrus and other sour fruits (such as strawberries and rhubarb), sugar, red meats, pork products and alcohol. Other foods can positively help your arthritic body – such saviours include artichokes, parsley, asparagus, broccoli, cabbage and other brassicas, chicory and turnips. Nutrient-rich broths with plenty of cabbage, celery and carrots provide vital sustenance for bone and cartilage, and aid the body's continual repair of joint wear and tear.

### dr jarvis' arthritis cure

A traditional recipe from Vermont, USA, this sweet and sour combination should be drunk regularly to enhance health. By correcting the pH balance in your body and cleansing the system of toxins, cider vinegar helps to relieve aches and pains. It also improves the metabolism of calcium in the body. The relaxing effects of honey add further pain-relieving properties.

*1 dessertspoon cider vinegar*
*1 teaspoon honey*
*250ml (8fl oz) hot water*

Add the vinegar and honey to a cup of hot water and drink in the evening before going to bed. 1 serving

## cabbage cooler

A hot scrumptious soup that cools the heat generated in arthritic joints. Thick, creamy and full of delicious crunchy vegetables, this soup will give you a wealth of nutrients to help repair wear and tear in the joints. In particular, cabbage cleanses toxins and clears uric acid from the system and makes a good anti-inflammatory.

*1 tablespoon olive oil*
*2 medium onions, peeled and sliced*
*3 medium carrots, washed and diced*
*2 sticks of celery, washed and sliced*
*1 medium leek, washed and sliced thinly*
*1.2 litres (2 pints) vegetable or chicken stock*
*salt and freshly ground pepper*
*1 medium cabbage, shredded*
*300ml (½ pint) cream or natural yogurt*
*fresh parsley, to garnish*

Heat the oil in a saucepan, add the vegetables, except the cabbage, and stir over a low heat for 5-10 minutes. Add the stock and seasoning, cover, and bring to the boil then reduce the heat and simmer for 30 minutes. Cook the cabbage in a little water for 5 minutes until slightly softened. Add to the soup with half the cream (or yogurt) and heat gently. Serve topped with the remainder of the cream (or yogurt) and garnished with parsley. 4 servings

## egyptian joint juice

Famous since the days of the Pharaohs for soothing aches and pains, this juice combines the contrasting tastes of aromatic celery and sweet carrot. This savoury duo provides a wonderful drink for all inflammatory joint conditions. Both celery and carrots are rich in nutrients for repairing joints and contain the antioxidant vitamins A and C which help prevent degenerative disease. They also aid digestion and cleanse the system of toxins and uric acid.

*125ml (4fl oz) celery juice*
*250ml (8fl oz) carrot juice*
*3 sprigs parsley*
*salt and freshly ground pepper*

Blend all the ingredients together in a liquidizer.
1 serving

## anaemia

If you are feeling tired, down in the dumps, perhaps irritable, or if you are suffering from headaches, dizziness or breathlessness, you may be anaemic. It is important to establish the cause of your anaemia to remedy the problem effectively. If your diet is low in iron or folic acid, drinks made from green leafy vegetables and herbs will boost your intake. Apricots and prunes are rich in iron, while tomatoes, watercress and spinach contain a wealth of both iron and folic acid. To ensure proper absorption of these nutrients a healthy digestion is vital. Drinking tea, coffee and alcohol can all impair absorption, as can a deficiency of vitamin E.

### orange and prune blood-builder

*The sweet velvet-textured prune blends well with the sharpness of the orange juice, to produce a delicious sweet and sour remedy for anaemia. The rich vitamin C content of the orange perfectly enhances the absorption of iron from the prunes. By restoring the natural balance of bacteria in the stomach and bowel, and enhancing absorption, both the yogurt and cinnamon help to ensure your digestion makes the best of this iron-rich tonic.*

*6 prunes (stones removed)*
*100ml (3½fl oz) fresh orange juice*
*1 tablespoon natural live yogurt*
*a pinch of ground cinnamon*

Blend the prunes, orange juice and yogurt together in a liquidizer. Drink sprinkled with cinnamon. 1 serving

### watercress, spinach and tomato pick-me-up

*The rich dark-green colour of this amazing tonic could almost have you feeling better by just looking at it, knowing that it is full to bursting with nutrients to restore your energy and strength. The high vitamin C content of the watercress, spinach, tomatoes and lemon juice will help ensure absorption of their iron and folic acid content, aided by the vitamin E also found in watercress. The pungency of the Worcestershire sauce and cayenne pepper adds a delightful bite to the recipe, meanwhile boosting digestion and absorption.*

*500g (1lb) ripe tomatoes, skinned*
*4 large spinach leaves, washed*
*½ bunch watercress, washed*
*1 teaspoon soy sauce*
*2 teaspoons lemon juice*
*1 tablespoon Worcestershire sauce*
*a pinch of cayenne pepper*
*sea salt to taste*
*5 ice cubes*
*a pinch of thyme, to garnish*

Blend all the ingredients together in a liquidizer. Strain and serve garnished with thyme. 3-4 servings

## chinese apricot and grapefruit tonic

*To the Chinese both apricots and grapefruit have a sweet-and-sour flavour. Apricots have a reputation as an energy tonic, while grapefruit benefits the stomach and restores the harmony of stomach chi. Honey is eaten by the Chinese to improve digestion and for anaemia. The iron in the apricots and the folic acid and vitamin C in the grapefruit combine to make this delicious thirst-quenching drink an ideal remedy for those who are run down or anaemic.*

4-6 dried apricots
2 teaspoons honey
300ml (½ pint) grapefruit juice
a sprinkling of ground nutmeg

Cook the apricots in enough water to cover, until soft. Drain. Stir in the honey while the apricots are hot. Add the grapefruit juice and liquidize. Sprinkle with nutmeg before drinking.

1 serving

# cold hands and feet

Poor circulation may make you feel the cold more than others, especially in your extremities. You may look pale and be prone to problems such as chilblains, low energy, sluggish digestion and constipation, particularly in winter. People with poor circulation may be born with it or else it can be related to stress and tension, a sedentary lifestyle, a weak or aging heart, or hardening of the arteries.

Take plenty of exercise to move the blood and strengthen the heart. Avoid smoking as it constricts the blood vessels and encourages plaque to form in your arteries, thereby slowing the circulation. Restrict your tea and coffee intake as they also constrict your blood vessels and exacerbate tension. Try to keep warm in cold weather and do not wear tight clothes as they will impede blood flow.

When it comes to food and drink, the best thing you can do is avoid anything cold. Lovely hot soups with plenty of warming ingredients such as garlic, onions and leeks liberally spiced with ginger, cayenne or mustard to stimulate the circulation will warm you to the very ends of your fingers and toes. A steaming cup of ginger tea will do just as well whether you drink it or use it as a hot foot bath for 10 minutes. Ingredients rich in calcium, magnesium and vitamin E, such as nuts and seeds, whole grains and green leafy vegetables, relieve constriction in the blood vessels and improve blood flow.

Iron and vitamin C-rich foods like watercress, parsley, apricots, prunes and blackcurrants dilate the arteries and help prevent anaemia which increases sensitivity to cold. Omega-3 essential fatty acids such as those found in fatty fish, evening primrose oil and linseed oil improve the circulation and help to prevent fatty deposits in the arteries.

## zanzibar zinger

This exotic blend of tangy grapefruit and a medley of spices makes a wonderfully warming drink for a cold winter's day. Grapefruit is rich in vitamin C and bioflavonoids which dilate and strengthen the blood vessels and improve the circulation through them. Cloves, from the beautiful shores of Zanzibar (once the most important trade centre in East Africa), as well as cinnamon and nutmeg dilate the blood vessels and stimulate the heart and circulation.

*300ml (½ pint) grapefruit juice*
*3 cloves*
*1 cinnamon stick*
*1 tablespoon honey*
*nutmeg to taste*

Place the grapefruit juice, cloves and cinnamon in a pan and heat. Keep the mixture almost at simmering point for 5 minutes. Remove from the heat and strain. Stir in the honey and sprinkle with a dash of nutmeg. 1 serving

## french onion soup

One of the most inviting soups imaginable, especially on a cold winter's night, when it comes steaming hot from the grill, the melted cheese bubbling over the top. The French certainly know how to cook and how to warm not only the cockles of your heart but also those cold extremities. With their pungent warming properties, onions have the ability to stimulate the circulation, dilate the arteries, lower blood pressure, reduce harmful cholesterol levels and help guard against heart attacks.

*1 tablespoon olive oil*
*6 onions, peeled and sliced into thin rings*
*4 garlic cloves, thinly slivered*
*1 teaspoon sugar*
*1 tablespoon plain flour*
*1.2 litres (2 pints) vegetable or chicken stock*
*1 tablespoon fresh thyme*
*1 tablespoon fresh rosemary*
*salt and freshly ground pepper*
*1 French baguette*
*175g (6oz) Gruyère cheese, grated*

Heat the oil in a large pan over a low heat. Add the onions and cook for about 30 minutes. Add the garlic and cook for another minute or so. Then stir in the sugar and flour and cook for 1-2 minutes until the onions turn golden. Stir in the stock, bring to the boil and simmer, covered, for 45 minutes. Add the thyme, rosemary and seasoning.

While the soup is cooking, cut the French bread into 2.5cm (1in) slices and bake in an oven preheated to 180°C (350°F, gas mark 4) for about 20 minutes, turning once, until lightly golden. Place 4 ovenproof crocks on a baking sheet and ladle in the soup to 1cm (½in) from the rim. Float a piece of bread on the top of each bowl and cover well with grated cheese. Place under a hot grill until the cheese is golden brown and bubbling. Serve immediately. 4 servings

# blood pressure

Many people from their middle years onward suffer from raised blood pressure; it is estimated that high blood pressure affects one fifth of all adults in the Western world. You may have a hereditary tendency to high or low blood pressure which you can learn to adjust to. If you are overweight this will increase your tendency to high blood pressure, as will smoking and too much alcohol.

A good look at your diet and lifestyle may provide some answers to your blood pressure problems. An abundance of fresh fruit and vegetables, plenty of pulses, nuts and seeds, some fatty fish and tofu, will boost your intake of potassium, calcium and magnesium, all precious minerals for regulating blood pressure. If you treat yourself on a regular basis to drinks containing these and specific foods such as garlic, onions, beans and celery with an ability to lower blood pressure, you would certainly be doing your arteries some favours. It is worth noting that vegetarians have less incidence of high blood pressure than meat eaters.

Stress may play a part so it is always a good idea to replace caffeinated drinks, which exacerbate tension, with relaxing herbal teas such as chamomile, lemon balm or limeflower. Regular aerobic exercise, for 20-30 minutes a day, will not only help you to feel better generally, but also serve to regulate your blood pressure and keep your heart and arteries healthy.

## french garlic soup

If, like the French, you love garlic, then this pungent herby soup is an exquisitely pleasurable way to take a medicine for high blood pressure. For centuries all over the world, garlic has been believed to lower blood pressure. It reduces harmful cholesterol, opens the arteries and improves blood flow through them, helping to reduce heart attacks and strokes. The addition of coriander, parley and lemon juice tastes like a stroke of genius and may even reduce the antisocial effects of garlic by sweetening your breath.

*1 tablespoon olive oil*
*2 onions, peeled and sliced*
*900ml (1½ pints) vegetable or chicken stock*
*1 head of garlic, cloves peeled*
*1 tablespoon chopped coriander leaves*
*1 tablespoon chopped parsley leaves*
*salt and freshly ground pepper*
*1 tablespoon lemon juice*

Heat the oil in a saucepan and cook the onions for 5 minutes. Add the stock, garlic, two thirds of the herbs, and seasoning. Bring to the boil and simmer, covered, for 20 minutes. Remove from the heat, blend and stir in the lemon juice. Return to the heat and adjust the seasoning. Garnish with the remaining herbs and serve. This soup is particularly good with herb bread.
4 servings

## spanish gazpacho

This chunky vegetable soup, traditionally eaten all over Spain, blends the pungency of raw onions and garlic with the tang of tomatoes and lemon delightfully. The ingredients may vary slightly from one region to another but it is always served ice-cold. Garlic and olive oil taken on a regular basis have been shown to significantly lower blood pressure. The basil in pesto has a wonderfully relaxing effect, which helps to reduce stress levels, while the antioxidant vitamins abundant in peppers, tomatoes and cucumber help to protect the heart and arteries from disease.

½ medium cucumber
1 large onion
3 garlic cloves
3 tomatoes, chopped
2 tablespoons olive oil
2 tablespoons white wine vinegar
1 tablespoon lemon juice
1 dessertspoon tomato purée
1 teaspoon pesto sauce
1 green pepper, chopped very finely
700ml (1¼ pints) tomato juice
salt and freshly ground pepper
croutons or garlic bread to serve

Coarsely grate the cucumber into a large bowl, or dice for a more chunky soup. Blend the onion, garlic and tomatoes in a liquidizer or food processor (or grate the onion and garlic and finely chop the tomatoes). Add the oil, vinegar, lemon juice, tomato purée and pesto. Add this mixture to the cucumber with the green pepper. Add the tomato juice and season. Cover and chill thoroughly for about 6 hours. Serve with garlic bread or croutons and freshly ground pepper. 4 servings

## hawthorn and limeflower tea

This light, sweet and astringent-tasting tisane combines two of the best herbal remedies for reducing blood pressure. The honey-flavoured limeflowers reduce tension levels in the body and relax the arteries, while hawthorn leaves and flowers regulate the diameter of the arteries and soften deposits inside the artery walls. Hawthorn also helps to reduce stress and anxiety and can be used as a balancer for both high and low blood pressure.

1 teaspoon hawthorn (flowers and leaves)
1 teaspoon limeflowers
250ml (8fl oz) boiling water

Place the herbs in a pot and pour over boiling water. Cover and leave to infuse for 10 minutes. Drink a cupful 3 times daily. 1 serving

# constipation

If you are prone to constipation it may be that your diet lacks sufficient fibre provided by whole grains and a plentiful supply of vegetables and fruit. A combination of low-fibre foods and red meats can also upset the bacterial population of the gut and predispose to constipation. Drinks abundant in fibrous fruits such as bananas and apricots combined with live yogurt to re-establish the normal gut population can go a long way to remedy the problem. Regular exercise will also help to keep the bowels regular, while stress and tension can serve to contract the bowel and aggravate constipation.

## indian mango, peach and grape nectar

*This succulent energy-giving drink is not only a delight to the taste buds but also a wonderfully luxurious way to keep your bowels regular. Mango, with its soft fragrant flesh containing plenty of fibre and antioxidants, is popular in Ayurvedic medicine to cure constipation and as a rejuvenator. Similarly the sweet juicy peach has a gently laxative action. Grapes are well known for their cleansing action brought about by their ability to stimulate the liver and bowels.*

*1 mango, peeled and sliced*
*2 peaches, peeled and sliced*
*100g (4oz) white grapes*
*300ml (½ pint) milk*
*½ teaspoon ground cinnamon*

Blend all the ingredients together in a liquidizer until smooth and serve.
1 serving

## hungarian beetroot and carrot cleanser

*This sweet, blood-red vegetable juice is packed with health-giving nutrients and has the ability to nourish and cleanse at the same time. Fresh beetroot juice is particularly popular in Eastern Europe for its great detoxifying properties. By stimulating liver and bowel functions, it enhances the elimination of toxins and wastes and naturally makes a good remedy for constipation. Carrots similarly promote bowel activity and by soothing the lining of the gut help to cure constipation related to irritation or inflammation of the digestive tract.*

*3 large carrots, washed*
*2 medium-sized beetroot, washed*
*chopped fresh coriander leaves, to garnish*

Put the vegetables through a juicer and serve immediately, garnished with coriander. 1 serving

## greek almond regulator

*Thick, smooth and creamy, this sweet blend of fruit, nuts and yogurt not only provides an answer to sluggish bowels but is also enjoyed by the Greeks as a meal in itself. Eaten regularly, bananas and almonds are ideal for promoting normal bowel function because they contain plenty of fibre. Being calming foods, they are helpful when constipation is related to nervous tension. Oranges have a laxative effect, while the yogurt helps regulate the bowels.*

*2 ripe bananas, peeled and chopped*
*50g (2oz) ground almonds*
*150ml (¼ pint) fresh orange juice*
*150ml (¼ pint) Greek natural yogurt*
*1 tablespoon honey*
*a pinch of ground nutmeg*

Place all the ingredients in a blender and blend to a smooth creamy consistency. Serve sprinkled with nutmeg. 1 serving

# heartburn

That uncomfortable feeling of fullness, bloating, tightness or even pain in the stomach or chest is familiar to many. It tends to happen soon after a meal, particularly when we are hurried, stressed and tense, or when we eat on the run or rush about immediately after eating. The stomach muscles do not have a chance to relax, the digestive juices do not flow properly and as a result food is not properly broken down, nor does it move normally through the digestive tract to be assimilated and the residues eliminated. Often the acid contents of the stomach will move up rather than down causing that awful burning sensation in the chest we know as heartburn as the acid burns the lining of the oesophagus. After a while the stomach lining may become irritated and then chronically hot and inflamed and this can eventually give rise to ulcers. The muscles of the cardiac sphincter that separates the stomach from the oesophagus weaken and easily allow the acid contents of the stomach into the oesophagus so that indigestion and heartburn become chronic.

There are of course other culprits that give rise to indigestion and heartburn. Certain foods like chilli, chocolate, acidic foods like pickles, citrus fruits, pastries and fatty foods, smoking cigarettes, drinking coffee and alcohol can all increase acidity and irritate the stomach and weaken the cardiac sphincter. Pregnant women tend to suffer as higher hormone levels relax the muscles of the sphincter. The tendency to heartburn is further aggravated as the growing baby pushes up against the stomach. Heartburn is also a symptom of hiatus hernia which is most common in people who are overweight.

For the most part simple changes in diet and lifestyle will remedy the situation. If you make soups and other drinks using herbs such as cardamom, aniseed, chamomile, mint, fennel, coriander and caraway these will help to relax the stomach, improve digestion and relieve pain and discomfort. Cooling and soothing foods like yogurt, ripe bananas, beetroot, cabbage and carrot will help to relieve irritation and heat.

Always sit in a relaxed fashion to eat and eat slowly, chewing each mouthful thoroughly. Do not get up, bend over or lie down straight after eating, and give your stomach around an hour to digest before taking exercise. Eat regularly but try not to overload your stomach by eating large meals as they take a long time to digest and allow more opportunity for the stomach contents to irritate and to move upward into the oesophagus. It is best not to eat anything for two to three hours before going to bed so that the stomach should be empty before you lie down and so not cause heartburn.

## french chamomile and mint tisane

The French, who can be particularly preoccupied about the health of their livers and stomachs, make a habit of drinking herbal tisanes following a meal. Chamomile and mint are great favourites for the digestion and are delightfully refreshing. Both these herbs are excellent for relaxing tension in the stomach muscles and for relieving heat, irritation and inflammation of the stomach lining. Meadowsweet is one of the best herbal antacids

*2 teaspoons dried chamomile flowers*
*2 teaspoons dried spearmint leaves*
*2 teaspoons dried meadowsweet*
*600ml (1 pint) water*

Place the herbs in a teapot and pour over boiling water. Cover and leave to infuse for 10-15 minutes. Drink a cupful three times daily, after meals, or more frequently if necessary to relieve the symptoms. 2-3 servings

### caribbean cure

A luscious drink of West Indian fruits to bring a hint of tropical paradise and settle your stomach at the same time. The sweet coconut milk is excellent for relieving acidity, the tangy pineapple is a wonderful anti-inflammatory and contains an enzyme bromelain, which helps balance stomach acid. Similarly the juicy papaya cools and soothes and also contains papain, a remarkable enzyme which can break down protein and so help your own stomach enzymes to digest food.

*½ ripe papaya (or 10 dried pieces if fresh*
  *is not available)*
*3 thick slices fresh or tinned pineapple*
*300ml (½ pint) coconut milk*
*sparkling or still mineral water, to dilute*
  *(optional)*
*a pinch of ground nutmeg*

If using dried papaya, cook it in a little water until soft, then drain. Place the papaya, pineapple and coconut milk in a liquidizer and blend until smooth. Dilute with a little water if you like. Add a pinch of nutmeg and take a glassful three times daily after meals. 1-2 servings

### licorice and mandarin peel tea

The exotic combination of licorice and mandarin makes an ideal recipe for digestive disorders. Licorice has healing and soothing effects on the stomach and allays heat and inflammation associated with heartburn. Through its affinity with the adrenal glands licorice increases the ability to withstand stress and mandarin peel eases its digestion.

*5g (⅙oz) dried licorice root*
*5g (⅙oz) dried mandarin peel*
*600ml (1 pint) water*

Place the ingredients in a pan, bring to the boil and simmer for 20 minutes. Strain and drink a cupful twice daily. 2-3 servings

# flatulence

A certain amount of intestinal gas is normal, but when it becomes excessive it can cause uncomfortable bloating and embarrassment. Sometimes the pain it causes is severe and can be mistaken for more serious abdominal problems. Occasional flatulence is probably due to eating wind-promoting foods – beans and pulses, brassicas such as broccoli and Brussels sprouts, pastries and artichokes. Bacteria in the bowel start to digest these foods and in the process produce wind. To help you avoid this, soak dried beans for 12 hours before cooking them in fresh water, and add digestive herbs and spices such as cumin, caraway, ginger and coriander.

More chronic wind may come from a weak digestion or from eating foods that do not agree with you. There are several herbal teas that could improve things. Mint, basil, chamomile, lemon balm, lemon grass, rosemary, cinnamon, aniseed, marjoram and thyme all stimulate the flow of digestive juices and enhance digestion as well as relax tension in the bowel. Many people have difficulty digesting wheat products such as bread and pastry; others have problems with milk products due to a lactose intolerance. It may be well worth eliminating one or other of these from your diet for a trial period of a month.

There are other factors which can predispose to flatulence. If you eat too fast or in a tense emotional state, your digestion will suffer and you are less likely to digest your food properly. You may have a tendency to swallow air, especially if you chew gum or consume a lot of carbonated drinks. It is quite common to experience flatulence and bloating when on antibiotics. When the balance of the bacterial population in the gut is disturbed it gives an opportunity for yeast to proliferate and this in turn gives rise to wind. The best way to remedy this is to go on a yeast-free diet and eat plenty of foods that help to re-establish the beneficial bacteria in the gut such as olive oil, garlic and live yogurt (see Candidiasis, p. 118).

## indian sweet lassi

This traditional Eastern beverage tastes out of this world with its exotic blend of sweet rose water and honey and pungent spices. Live yogurt, rose water and honey all enhance digestion and help to balance the bacterial population in the gut. Cardamom and cinnamon act similarly and at the same time stimulate the flow of digestive juices and relieve tension throughout the digestive tract that might inhibit proper digestion.

*225g (8oz) natural live yogurt*
*150ml (¼ pint) rose water*
*1 tablespoon honey*
*½ teaspoon ground cardamom*
*½ teaspoon ground cinnamon*

Combine all the ingredients together, stirring well, and serve. 1 serving

## west african lemon grass tea

Herbal teas are very popular in Mali where this exquisite lemon-flavoured local favourite is served from ornate brass teapots with long spouts into little cups with no handles. Lemon grass is an excellent preventative and remedy for flatulence. It stimulates digestion and relieves tension in the gut. Its valuable anti-fungal properties help overcome any overgrowth of yeast that might give rise to wind.

*25g (1oz) lemon grass*
*600ml (1 pint) boiling water*

Place the lemon grass in a teapot and pour over boiling water. Leave to infuse for 20 minutes and drink hot after meals. **2-3 servings**

## guadaloupe grapefruit gas reliever

This zingy blend of tropical fruit juices makes a lovely refreshing drink for a hot day and combines three of the best foods for improving digestion and dispelling flatulence. Grapefruit helps the digestion, particularly of starchy foods and fats, and clears waste products from the bowel. Mango will settle a nervous stomach and, like pineapple, enhances digestion and regulates the bowels.

*1 ripe mango, peeled and sliced*
*175g (6oz) fresh or tinned pineapple*
*juice of ½ pink grapefruit*
*fresh lemon balm leaves, to garnish*

Place the ingredients in a blender and blend until smooth. Serve garnished with lemon balm.
1 serving

# colic

When the muscular walls of the abdomen contract they cause acute spasms of pain that can last for minutes or hours. Young babies, up to the age of about three months, seem to be particularly prone to colic causing them to cry, often inconsolably, and to draw up their legs when the spasms occur. There may be a variety of contributory factors including the immaturity of the digestive tract, swallowing air, overfeeding, intolerance to milk formulae or particles of food substances coming through breast milk, constipation or even parental stress. The causes may lie outside the abdomen and relate more to cranial pressure brought about by the birth.

Children and adults can also suffer from colic which is often related to wind, indigestion or infection. Stress can be a major contributory factor here, causing tension and spasm in the stomach and interrupting the normal process of digestion. Some foods may irritate the lining of the walls of the digestive tract, causing the muscles to go into spasm and thereby leading to acute pain. What is needed most to relieve the pain in the short term is a drink that relaxes spasm in the stomach muscles. If it contains substances to soothe an irritated gut and to enhance the normal process of digestion, so much the better.

Gripe water made predominantly from dill seed, is an old-fashioned favourite for babies' colic. In the 1950s and 1960s it was given as a preventative measure to babies after each feed. Both dill and fennel seeds are excellent remedies for colic as they relax tension in the muscles of the digestive tract, release wind and enhance digestion. Where stress and tension appear to be the problem, chamomile and catmint will relax mind and body and have a particular affinity for the stomach.

## chamomile and fennel seed tea

This pleasant, mild-tasting herbal tea is ideal for babies' colic. The distinctive flavour of chamomile, which is not everybody's cup of tea, is nicely disguised by the distinctive yet sweet taste of fennel. As well as relieving tension and spasm, both these aromatic herbs have antiseptic properties, so that if colic is related to infection this tea will help speed it on its way. Where colic is caused by irritation of the stomach lining the anti-inflammatory effects of chamomile are perfect.

½ teaspoon fennel seeds
1 teaspoon dried chamomile flowers
250ml (8fl oz) boiling water

Crush the fennel seeds, using a mortar and pestle, and place in a teapot with the chamomile. Pour on boiling water and leave to infuse for 10 minutes. Dilute with four parts warm water for babies and give two tablespoons in a bottle or on a spoon before feeding and again afterward if the baby seems uncomfortable. For children and adults serve undiluted or mixed with warm water to taste. 1 serving

## danish carrot and dill soup

Simple sweet carrots mixed in Danish fashion with garlic and dill not only transform this soup into something exiting but also a perfect remedy for children and adults alike, to soothe the stomach, enhance digestion and release wind and spasm. The humble carrot provides nutrition for the nervous system and increases our resilience to stress. It soothes the mucous membranes throughout the digestive tract helping to reduce irritation.

1 tablespoon olive oil
2 medium garlic cloves, peeled and
   chopped finely
1 large onion, peeled and sliced thinly
450g (1lb) carrots, washed and sliced
2 large potatoes, washed and sliced
600ml (1 pint) vegetable or chicken stock
salt and freshly ground pepper
2 tablespoons chopped fresh dill

Heat the oil in a medium-sized pan. Add the garlic and onion and stir over a low heat until the onion is tender. Add the carrots, potatoes and stock. Bring to the boil and simmer for about 30 minutes, until the vegetables are cooked. Blend until smooth. Season with salt and pepper and 1 tablespoon of the dill. Garnish with the remaining dill when serving. 4 servings

## chamomile and catmint tea

A light aromatic tisane that makes a perfect relaxing remedy to relieve a tense stomach and banish colic. Both chamomile and catmint relieve tightness and spasm in the smooth muscle throughout the digestive tract. Through their sedative action on the central nervous system they relieve stress that may contribute to such tension. They also have the ability to reduce any irritation and inflammation of the gut lining and to resolve infection that may give rise to colic.

1 teaspoon fresh or dried chamomile flowers
2 teaspoons fresh or 1 teaspoon dried catmint
600ml (1 pint) water

Place the herbs in a teapot and pour over boiling water. Cover and leave to infuse for 10-15 minutes. Drink warm every hour or so to relieve the symptoms. 2-3 servings

# diarrhoea

Acute diarrhoea usually means you have a bowel infection and your body is doing its best to rid itself quickly of the toxins causing it. Ideally you should allow diarrhoea to run its course, taking care to replace lost fluids and electrolytes by drinking plenty of liquids with honey. Drinks containing ingredients such as rice, pear and mango to soothe the gut, lemon and blueberries to combat infection and yogurt to restore the normal bacterial population of the gut are ideal. A more chronic problem may be related to infection, bowel disease or food allergy and requires medical investigation.

## caribbean calmer

*This sweet creamy drink tastes almost like nectar and is the next best thing to a meal when you may not feel like eating solid food. Pears and mangoes are wonderfully thirst-quenching and calm an irritated gut. Women in the West Indies know all about the binding and soothing nature of mashed bananas, the first food they think of when their children have diarrhoea. Bananas reduce the level of harmful bacteria in the gut and their high level of natural sugars is ideal to replace those lost through diarrhoea. Cinnamon is highly antiseptic and will help to fight off infection.*

75g (3oz) fresh mango
1 large or 2 small pears
1 banana
200ml (7fl oz) rice milk
a pinch of ground cinnamon

Blend the fruit and rice milk together in a liquidizer and serve sprinkled with cinnamon.
1 serving

## romany raspberry cure

*Raspberries must be unrivalled in sweetness and delicacy of flavour by any other soft fruit and make a sumptuous treat for a hot summer's day. By toning the lining of the digestive tract, raspberries have an astringent effect and protect the gut from irritation and inflammation. They contain natural antibiotics that help fight off infecting organisms in the gut as does honey which has deservedly won a place in the World Health Organization's recipe to cure travellers' diarrhoea.*

100g (4oz) fresh or frozen
  raspberries
2 tablespoons Greek natural yogurt
1 tablespoon honey
2 tablespoons milk

Blend all the ingredients together and drink. 1 serving

## american blueberry tea

This tangy blend of blueberries and lemons, put together easily in seconds, tastes great and with its blue-purple colour looks inviting. Its antiseptic and astringent properties make this tea one of the most popular American folk remedies for diarrhoea and infection in the gut. The high concentrations of antiviral and antibacterial compounds found in both blueberries and lemons explain their ability to ward off infection, notably E. coli, the bacteria most commonly associated with diarrhoea.

  1 tablespoon blueberry jam
  1 teaspoon honey
  1 teaspoon lemon juice
  300ml (½ pint) boiling water

Place the jam, honey and lemon juice in a large mug. Pour on boiling water, stirring to dissolve the jam. Cover and allow to infuse for 5 minutes before drinking. 1 serving

# diverticulitis

Diverticulitis occurs when small sacs or pockets, known as diverticula, form on the walls of the bowel in weakened areas. These tend to develop in people over the age of 50 after years of pressure in the bowel caused by trying to pass hard, dry stools. Those who suffer from chronic constipation are particularly prone to diverticular disease and the underlying cause of this is lack of dietary fibre and insufficient exercise. Sometimes people with this problem have no or very mild symptoms, others suffer from alternating diarrhoea and constipation, flatulence and sometimes pain in the lower left side of the abdomen. If particles of faecal matter become trapped in the little sacs or outpouchings they can set up inflammation and become infected, giving rise to diverticulitis. This can be characterized by abdominal cramps, fever and rectal bleeding.

The solution to this problem is first and foremost to change your diet. Incorporate plenty of whole grains, fruit and vegetables, which are all high in fibre. It is important to drink plenty of liquid – six to eight glasses a day – to help regulate the bowels and remedy constipation (see also Constipation, p. 100). Drinks made from fruits such as pineapple and papaya are especially therapeutic as they contain proteolytic enzymes which aid digestion and help to prevent diverticular disease. Pears, potatoes, rice, barley and millet are all excellent as they cool an inflamed gut. Carrot, cabbage, lettuce, spinach and turnips in vegetable juices and puréed soups are also beneficial as they also soothe inflammation and regulate the bowels.

Caffeinated drinks are best avoided as they tend to cause contraction in the bowel and create more pressure, thus aggravating the problem. Avoid eating refined carbohydrates, such as white flour products, and foods that contain hard particles such as nuts and seeds, including seeds contained in fruits like raspberries, blackberries and tomatoes, and vegetables like cucumber, because they can become lodged in the little sacs and aggravate diverticulitis. Remember to take plenty of exercise.

## american papaya and almond dream

In America diverticular disease is a huge problem, with about half the population over the age of 60 suffering from the disease. This thick, creamy and really luscious combination of laxative and soothing fruits and cooling, anti-inflammatory rice milk will calm an inflamed bowel. If drunk regularly it will keep the bowels moving and thus remedy the problem.

*6 fresh or dried apricots*
*50g (2oz) fresh or dried papaya (ready soaked)*
*300ml (½ pint) rice milk*
*1 tablespoon ground almonds*
*a pinch of ground or freshly grated root ginger*

If using dried apricots, cook them in a little water until soft and drain. Place the ingredients together in a blender and blend until smooth. Serve sprinkled with a little ginger. 1 serving

## middle eastern pear and melon nectar

The blend of these most succulent of fruits tastes really like pure nectar and provides a delightful way to remedy your bowel problems. Both pears and melons are well known in the Middle East for their cooling and soothing properties, particularly in the digestive tract where they not only relieve inflammation but also help to keep the bowels regular.

*½ ripe Cantaloupe melon*
*3 ripe pears, peeled and with cores removed*

Blend the pears and melon together in the blender and serve. For a slight variation and a more exotic flavour, add a little coconut milk.
1 serving

## medieval parsnip and swede soup

Medieval English monks grew parsnips in their monastery gardens as they were considered vital for providing sustenance on the days when eating meat was forbidden. Sweet and starchy, parsnips and swede blended together make a thick, nourishing soup which is high in fibre. It is ideal for keeping the bowels regular and for preventing as well as relieving diverticular disease.

*1 tablespoon olive oil*
*1 onion, diced*
*2 small potatoes, diced*
*2 large parsnips, diced*
*1 small swede, diced*
*900ml (1½ pints) vegetable*
*  or chicken stock*
*salt and freshly ground pepper*
*450ml (¾ pint) milk*
*1 tablespoon soy sauce*
*fresh coriander leaves, to garnish*

Fry the vegetables in the olive oil gently for 5 minutes. Add the stock and bring to the boil. Cover and simmer for 30 minutes until the vegetables are soft. Add salt and pepper to taste. Blend with the milk and soy sauce and serve garnished with coriander. 4-6 servings

# irritable bowel syndrome

Irritable bowel syndrome (IBS) is the most common gastro-intestinal problem presented to doctors in the West. It is characterized by either diarrhoea or constipation, or both, flatulence and distension, and often abdominal pain. IBS may be related to diet, stress, weak digestion, food intolerance, particularly to wheat or milk products, and excess candida in the gut.

Eat plenty of fibre, preferably from fruits, vegetables and pulses rather than cereals. Soups made from cooked vegetables such as carrots, leeks, cabbage, parsnip and celery will not only provide fibre but also a wealth of nutrients. Raw vegetables can stress the bowel while it is not functioning well. Add aromatic herbs (dill, peppermint, fennel, lemon balm) and warming spices (ginger, cinnamon, caraway, cumin) to these soups to enhance digestion and relax any tension and spasm in the gut. Fruit drinks from apples, pears, apricots, pineapple, papaya and peaches aid digestion and help regulate your bowels.

Antifungal herbs such as garlic, thyme and oregano help to combat an overgrowth of candida in the bowel. Drinks containing live yogurt help re-establish the normal bacterial population in the gut after frequent use of antibiotics. Avoid caffeinated and carbonated drinks.

## malaysian papaya and coconut dream

This exotic mixture of Far Eastern delights combines the sweetness of papaya, honey and coconut with the sharpness of limes and the result is mouth-wateringly good. The papaya enhances digestion while soothing the gut. The limes and honey help to balance the bacterial population and regulate the bowels. The coconut milk is rich in B vitamins to nourish the nerves, and it reduces tension and calms irritation in the bowels.

*6 chunks fresh or dried papaya*
*juice of 1 lime*
*1 teaspoon honey*
*300ml (½ pint) coconut milk*
*sliced lime, to garnish*

If using dried papaya, cook in a little water until soft, then drain. Blend the papaya, lime juice, honey and coconut milk together in the blender, pour into a large glass and garnish with a slice of lime. 1 serving

## english chamomile and mint tea

The idea of sitting on an English lawn sipping chamomile and mint tea on a summer's afternoon immediately brings a sense of refreshment and ease. This light aromatic tisane is the very thing when stress and tension cause pain and irritation in the bowel. Chamomile is truly one of the best remedies for stress-related bowel problems and mint the ideal herb for releasing spasm in the gut.

*2 teaspoons fresh or 1 teaspoon dried chamomile flowers*
*2 teaspoons fresh or 1 teaspoon dried mint leaves*
*600ml (1 pint) water*

Place the herbs in a teapot and pour over boiling water. Cover and leave to infuse for 10-15 minutes. Drink a cupful regularly, three times a day, while symptoms persist. 2-3 servings

## chinese ginger and fennel congee

In China it is traditional to give congees, which are rice soups, to children, old people and those recovering from illness. Some Chinese just like to have them for breakfast. The rice is not only filling but also soothes inflammation and relaxes spasm in the digestive tract. The fennel and ginger promote digestion and absorption and their antispasmodic action also relieves tension and pain in the gut.

*1 tablespoon fennel seeds*
*200g (7oz) long grain white rice*
*4cm (1½in) piece of fresh root ginger, peeled and sliced thinly*
*3 litres (6 pints) water*
*1-2 drops sesame oil*
*soy sauce to taste*

Roast the fennel seeds in a dry skillet for a few minutes, stirring to prevent their burning, then crush with a mortar and pestle. Place with the rice, ginger and water in a large pan, cover and bring to the boil. Simmer on a low heat for about 1 hour and serve hot, seasoned with sesame oil and a little soy sauce. 8 servings

# haemorrhoids

Are you sitting comfortably? If not it may be that you, like about one third of people in the West, are suffering from haemorrhoids. Haemorrhoids, or piles, are varicose veins that form internally or externally in the anal region, which have become swollen. They can be uncomfortable, even painful, they may itch or burn, and tend to bleed. The best way to treat haemorrhoids is to avoid their developing in the first place and this means making sure you have plenty of fibre in your diet, you take regular aerobic exercise and do not get constipated (see also Constipation, p. 100). Help yourself by training your bowels, never ignore any urge to go and never strain while passing a motion. Try to avoid sitting or standing for long periods of time – sometimes piles can develop after a long car journey over a day or two.

Stress and anxiety can cause the muscles in the bowel to contract and lead to constipation. Herbs that relax the bowel such as chamomile, lemon balm, fennel and peppermint can be taken as hot teas and replace tea and coffee that only exacerbate stress and aggravate bowel problems.

Eat whole grains and fresh fruit and vegetables – around five portions of each every day – and drink plenty of fluid to keep your bowels regular. Aim to drink 2 litres (or 4 pints) a day. Carrots, beetroot, celery, peas and parsnips make good fibrous soups and vegetable juices, and citrus fruits, grapes, apricots, prunes and bananas are ideal for fruity drinks to prevent constipation. Yogurt helps to maintain a healthy bacterial population in the gut which also affects bowel movements. Make sure you include plenty of oily foods such as pumpkin, sesame and sunflower seeds, and virgin olive oil in your diet to lubricate the bowels.

## spanish zuma de frutas

Visitors to Spain will find a wonderful assortment of freshly squeezed fruit juices to quench their thirst and when served with ice they are exquisitely refreshing on a hot day. This combination of tangy citrus fruits and sweet grapes not only provides a feast for the taste buds but also has a beneficial effect on the digestion. By stimulating the liver and bowels these fruits have a cleansing effect and make a great remedy for constipation.

*100ml (3½fl oz) orange juice*
*100ml (3½fl oz) grapefruit juice*
*100ml (3½fl oz) grape juice*
*ice cubes (optional)*
*fresh mint or lemon balm, to garnish*

Blend the fruit juices together. Serve over ice on a hot day if you wish and add a few mint or lemon balm leaves when you serve. 1 serving

### russian relief

The Russians are very fond of both beetroot and yogurt in their cuisine and also for their well researched medicinal benefits. Live yogurt containing cultures of *Lactobacillus acidophilus* helps to combat putrefactive bacteria in the bowel that might otherwise predispose to constipation, while beetroot with its great cleansing effect stimulates the liver and bowels into action. Here their sweet taste blends well with the aromatic celery and mint.

*90ml (3fl oz) beetroot juice*
*45ml (1½fl oz) celery juice*
*45ml (1½tl oz) natural live yogurt*
*1 spring onion, chopped*
*fresh mint leaves*

Blend the vegetable juices with the yogurt. Garnish with a little spring onion and mint when serving. 1 serving

### scottish oatmeal and cinnamon mover

Traditional breakfast food in Scotland, oats contain plenty of fibre to bulk out the bowel contents and speed their passage through the system. Sweet, smooth and creamy, this oaty drink is enlivened by the spicy cinnamon and sharp lemon, and makes a great warmer for cold days. Both oats and cinnamon are great tonics to the nervous system, helping to relieve tension that might contribute to constipation and haemorrhoids.

*1 tablespoon coarse oatmeal*
*1.2 litres (2 pints) cold water*
*honey to taste*
*juice of ½ lemon*
*1 teaspoon ground cinnamon*

Place the oatmeal and water in a pan and simmer on a low heat for 1 hour. Sweeten with honey. Strain then add the lemon juice and cinnamon. Serve hot. 4 servings

# nausea

Distressing and debilitating, unsure whether you are about to vomit or not, nausea must be one of the most horrible sensations we experience. Unfortunately for many women, chronic nausea can accompany the first twelve weeks of pregnancy and often it is not just "morning sickness" – for many it can last all day. Nausea and vomiting can also be related to a variety of other things: an infection or intestinal parasites, a disturbance of the inner ear balance mechanism or travel sickness, overindulgence in food or alcohol, toxic overload of the liver, the effects of chemotherapy, or stress.

For some that terrible feeling of nausea is relieved by vomiting, but for others it can continue even when the contents of the stomach have been emptied several times. If this is the case, it is important that you drink plenty of liquid to prevent dehydration. Consult your doctor if persistent vomiting is accompanied by faintness, severe pain or fever.

Whatever the cause, one of the best and most delicious remedies for nausea is ginger. In a study in 1996, ginger effectively relieved motion sickness in 75 per cent of cases. Sipped as ginger tea, ginger beer or ginger ale it swiftly brings relief even when nausea is related to the toxic effects of chemotherapy. Drinks made from other aromatic spices like cinnamon, coriander, cumin and cardamom, and herbal teas including peppermint, fennel, dill and lemon verbena, can also be helpful. Not only do these settle the stomach, but also they all contain volatile oils which have powerful antimicrobial actions, effectively combating infection that can give rise to nausea and vomiting.

You may need to experiment a little when making drinks with herbs and spices to find which ones suit you best but it helps considerably if you like their taste. Moroccan mint tea (see p. 67) is highly recommended for it can swiftly relieve nausea. When nausea is related to emotional stress, try herbal teas that have calming properties as well as a beneficial effect on the digestion, such as lemon balm, chamomile, lavender and vervain.

## middle eastern stomach settler

This aromatic combination is popular in the Middle East for relieving nausea and apparently has been ever since the days of King Solomon, when the king's herbalist would grind the spices with a pestle and mortar to make this brew. Spices such as cinnamon and cardamom encourage the downward movement of energy in the digestive tract and so help to settle the stomach. Their highly antiseptic volatile oils are excellent for combating infection.

*3 small cinnamon sticks*
*   or one 15cm (6in) stick of cinnamon bark*
*1 teaspoon ground cardamom*
*250ml (8fl oz) hot water*

Grind the spices together in a coffee grinder. Place 1 teaspoon in a cup of hot water and sip slowly to bring relief. 1 serving

## lemon verbena and spearmint tea

If you sip this sweet, delicately flavoured tisane you will find that it helps to settle the stomach and calm nausea. The antiseptic volatile oils that give these herbs their exquisite taste and scent will help combat any infection, and the relaxing effect of the tea will calm tension and anxiety that may give rise to nausea. This drink's ability to promote normal digestion and absorption should soon have you feeling yourself again.

*1 teaspoon dried lemon verbena leaves*
*1 teaspoon dried or 2 teaspoons fresh*
*spearmint leaves*
*600ml (1 pint) water*

Place the herbs in a teapot and pour on boiling water. Cover and leave to infuse for 10-15 minutes. Sip ½ to 1 cupful when required.
2-4 servings

### ginger beer

Tasty and invigorating, ginger beer makes a refreshing, non-alcoholic, sparkling drink, warming in the winter, thirst-quenching in the summer. Cultivating the "plant" at home takes some commitment as it needs "feeding" every day but it is well worth the effort. Whatever the cause of nausea and vomiting, ginger is the best remedy, and it is perfectly safe to take throughout pregnancy. Sip ginger beer at intervals throughout the day whenever you feel queasy.

For the starter:
*15g (½oz) dried brewer's yeast*
*450ml (¾ pint) warm water*
*2 teaspoons ground ginger*
*2 teaspoons sugar*

To feed the "plant":
*6 teaspoons ground ginger*
*6 teaspoons sugar*

To make up:
*750g (1¾ lb) sugar*
*1.2 litres (2 pints) warm water*
*juice of 2 lemons*
*3 litres (5 pints) cold water*

Place the starter ingredients in a glass jar with a lid. Stir well, cover and put in a warm place, such as a sunny windowsill. Leave for 24 hours then "feed" daily for 6 days with 1 teaspoon ground ginger and 1 teaspoon sugar.

After 7 days strain the "plant" through a sieve. Dissolve the sugar in the warm water in a large bowl or jug. Add the lemon juice, cold water and the liquid from the "plant" and mix well. Bottle, in corked bottles, for at least seven days to mature. Serve with a sprig of fresh mint or lemon balm. Stored in a cool place, ginger beer will keep for about a week.

# candidiasis

Candida albicans is a yeast which lives harmlessly in all of us. If our normal immune mechanisms are inhibited and this yeast gets out of control, it can infest the mouth and throat, the digestive tract and the vagina. Drinks made from fruits and vegetables containing plenty of nutrients for the immune system will enhance the body's fight against the infection. Garlic, thyme, cinnamon and ginger added to drinks are excellent as they actually have antifungal properties. Foods containing yeast and sugar are best avoided.

## indian cucumber raita drink

*Cucumber and yogurt are traditionally eaten with hot curry in India as their cooling properties offset the heat of the spices. This drink is perfect for a hot summer's day and has the added benefit of being an excellent remedy for candidiasis. The yogurt helps to re-establish the normal bacterial population of the gut, thus holding yeast infection in check. The vitamins and minerals in cucumber help support the immune system, while the mint leaves contain essential oils with antifungal properties.*

*50g (2oz) cucumber, peeled and diced*
*90ml (3fl oz) natural live yogurt*
*90ml (3fl oz) milk*
*8-12 mint leaves*
*a squeeze of lime juice*
*salt to taste*
*a sprig of fresh mint and a slice of cucumber, to garnish*

Blend all the ingredients together in a liquidizer. Pour into a glass half filled with ice and garnish with mint and cucumber. 1 serving

## chinese mandarin and lychee cream

*This exotic blend of sweet lychee and tangy mandarin orange contains a wealth of vitamins, particularly vitamin C, to boost immunity. The Chinese eat lychees to benefit the digestion and relieve pain and irritation. Mandarins, lychees and yogurt are all taken to combat yeast infections, while the freshly grated ginger, which adds an unexpected bite to this delicious drink, provides extra antifungal properties.*

*100g (4oz) lychees, peeled (tinned if fresh not available)*
*150g (6oz) mandarin segments (tinned if fresh not available)*
*100ml (3½fl oz) natural live yogurt freshly grated ginger to taste*

Blend all the ingredients together in a liquidizer into a smooth cream. Garnish with a little fresh ginger and a couple of segments of mandarin.
1 serving

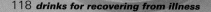

## french garlic syrup

The French herbalist Maurice Messegue said he was baptized with a clove of garlic on his lips. He, like other herbalists all over the world, praises garlic's powerful ability to combat a whole range of infections including fungal infections. In the intestines garlic regulates the flora and prevents harmful micro-organisms such as candida from proliferating there. So although this pungent syrup may not be everybody's cup of tea, it is nonetheless a brilliant remedy for candidiasis.

4 large garlic cloves, peeled and
  sliced thinly
2 teaspoons fresh or
  1 teaspoon dried thyme
about a dessertspoonful of
  runny honey

Place the garlic and thyme in a bowl and cover with honey. Leave for 2-3 hours. Crush to extract all the juice and strain. Take 1 teaspoon at least 3 times a day.

# premenstrual syndrome

There is a wide variety of symptoms that women can experience in the second half of the menstrual cycle which are loosely described as premenstrual syndrome (PMS). These can be mild or severe and include fluid retention, tender breasts, mood changes, fatigue, uterine cramping, headaches, clumsiness and poor concentration to name but a few. Apparently more than 150 premenstrual symptoms have been identified. Although many women accept these as normal, they certainly do not need to be suffered. On the contrary, there is plenty that you can do to help yourself.

PMS is primarily related to an imbalance of female hormones, in most cases an excess of oestrogen in relation to progesterone. It can often be precipitated by hormonal upheavals occurring at puberty, after pregnancy, when approaching the menopause or after taking the pill. Such hormonal imbalances are caused by a combination of physical, psychological and nutritional factors. Lack of exercise, a sluggish liver and low thyroid function can all play their part, as can stress and deficiencies of nutrients including vitamins A, B, E and C, magnesium, zinc, calcium and essential fatty acids.

Eating and drinking correctly is essential for maintaining our nutritional status, which in turn supports us physically and psychologically. Plenty of unrefined vegetable oils, nuts and seeds, whole grains, beans and pulses, fatty fish, and fresh fruit and vegetables will help maintain the right balance of hormones.

Tea, coffee, cocoa and chocolate are best avoided as the caffeine in them can interfere with hormone balance, by inhibiting the liver's breakdown of hormones once they have done their work. Alcohol needs to be kept to a minimum as it increases the body's need for B vitamins, magnesium, zinc and calcium, and stresses the liver, which in turn may interfere with hormone metabolism. As alternatives to these, make drinks containing ingredients that both prevent and treat PMS. Carrots, beetroot, watercress and other green leafy vegetables will all provide vitamin A. Kale, red peppers, bananas, avocados, mushrooms and nuts are rich in vitamin $B_6$, parsley, green vegetables, nuts and seeds contain magnesium and calcium, while soya beans, milk produce, nuts, seeds and avocados provide vitamin E.

### greek vitex tea

*Vitex agnus castus*, or chaste tree, is a beautiful shrub to be found all along the shores of the Aegean. In late summer you can harvest the highly aromatic seeds not only to make an exquisite tea but also to provide a perfect way to prevent and treat PMS. The seeds, which can be found in health-food shops and herbalists, have the amazing ability to stimulate and balance the function of the pituitary gland, and in particular to regulate its production of female sex hormones. The seeds can also be bought in health food shops and herbalists.

*25g (1oz) vitex seeds*
*600ml (1 pint) water*

Place the seeds and water in a pan and bring to the boil. Cover and simmer on a low heat for 15-20 minutes. Strain and drink a cupful each morning, half an hour before breakfast.
2-3 servings

## avocado dream

The smooth creamy taste and texture of the avocado and rice milk are bought to life by the bite and tang of the garlic, lemon juice and coriander to produce a drink that is definitely enough to satisfy any premenstrual food cravings! Avocados are ideal for those who suffer from PMS as they are rich in vitamins B and E for the hormonal system and, at the same time, they calm and strengthen the nervous system.

1 ripe avocado, peeled and sliced
1 garlic clove, peeled
juice of ½ lemon
300ml (½ pint) rice milk
salt and freshly ground pepper
a few sprigs of fresh coriander, to garnish

Place the avocado in a blender with the garlic, lemon juice and rice milk. Blend until smooth. Season with salt and pepper and serve garnished with fresh coriander. 1 serving

## chinese angelica tea

Chinese angelica is the most highly valued tonic herb for women in the East. It makes a deliciously sweet and mildly pungent tea which regulates hormones, and helps maintain normal function of the reproductive system. It is an ideal remedy to prevent and relieve PMS. It enhances circulation to and from the uterus, relieves period pains, stabilizes blood sugar, regulates the bowels, improves energy and calms the nerves.

25g (1oz) dried angelica root, sliced
600ml (1 pint) water

Place the herbs and water in a pan and bring to the boil. Simmer for 30 minutes, strain and drink a cupful twice daily. 2-3 servings

# cystitis

An acute bacterial infection in the urinary tract causes that most unpleasant sensation of never properly emptying your bladder and often, far worse, a feeling of passing broken glass when you urinate. Cystitis can also be associated with fever and abdominal pain and tends to affect women more frequently than men due to anatomical differences. Their shorter urethra provides an easy pathway for infection, normally *E. coli*, to travel to the bladder. Although many women suffer from chronic bladder infections, the symptoms are often not apparent and the infection may only come to light on routine urine analysis.

Clearly prevention is better than cure. If we drink 3-4 litres (6-8 pints) daily and regularly take substances into our bodies to combat infection and to flush toxins and bacteria out of the system, we need never suffer from cystitis.

Luckily there is a great variety of delicious ingredients that we can incorporate into drinks which will do just what we need both to prevent and treat bladder infections. Take cranberries, for example. These marvellous tart-tasting fruits contain substances that prevent bacteria from adhering to the walls of the urinary tract so that they are easily flushed out of the system without a chance to cause infection. Added to that, they contain arbutin, a constituent that has a diuretic effect and antiseptic properties. Live yogurt is another excellent preventative of bladder infections and makes lovely thick, smooth drinks with cooling and soothing properties. It makes sharp fruit juices more palatable and reduces the need for much sugar.

Carrots, celery, parsley and asparagus, with their diuretic and antiseptic properties, are also ideal for drinks such as soups and juices for the urinary system. Soups made with leeks, onions and garlic will all disinfect the bladder, while cucumber, courgettes, cabbage, pears and barley will cool and soothe an irritated bladder and relieve that burning pain.

## old english barley water

In Victorian England the traditional remedy for an inflamed bladder was a decoction of barley, often with a little added lemon which certainly enlivens what would otherwise be a rather bland-tasting drink. Barley was also given to invalids and convalescents to build up their strength. It has wonderfully cooling and soothing effects on the mucous membranes of the urinary tract to alleviate discomfort as well as diuretic properties to flush out infection. Lemons add their diuretic and antiseptic actions to maximize the benefits of this concoction.

*50g (2oz) unrefined pot barley*
*600ml (1 pint) boiling water*
*1½ tablespoons honey*
*juice of ½ lemon*

Place the barley and water in a pan and bring to the boil. Cover and simmer on a low heat for 30 minutes. Add the honey and stir well. Cool, strain and add the lemon juice. Drink lukewarm frequently through the day, depending on the severity of the symptoms. 2-3 servings

## american cranberry juice

Long popular as a folk remedy in North America for cystitis, cranberry juice has now been well researched for its ability to prevent and clear urinary infections. Native to America, cranberries make a beautiful pink-red drink but it is so tart that most people will want to sweeten it with sugar or honey. This does not detract from its effectiveness.

Drink 1 small glass (90ml/3fl oz) every day as a preventative, or 1 large glass (350ml/12fl oz) twice daily to treat an existing infection.

*450g (1lb) fresh cranberries (defrosted if frozen)*
*2 litres (3½ pints) water*
*honey or sugar to taste*
*natural live yogurt (optional)*

Place the cranberries in a large pan with the water and bring to the boil. Simmer on a low heat for 15-20 minutes until the liquid has reduced but is not syrupy. Remove from the heat and strain the liquid through a sieve. Stir in honey or sugar until it is sweet enough to drink. Leave to cool before drinking. This should keep in the refrigerator for 4-5 days. Stir in 1-2 teaspoons of live yogurt when serving if you like to make a smoother, less sour drink.

## carrot and parsley juice

The sweet, smooth taste of carrot blends well with the more pungent and aromatic parsley, to produce a very appetizing remedy for cystitis. The soothing and diuretic properties of carrots soon relieve irritation and inflammation of the bladder, while their antiseptic properties help to combat the infection. Parsley is also diuretic and highly antiseptic and its affinity for the urinary system makes it an excellent partner in this therapeutic duo.

*250ml (8fl oz) carrot juice*
*6 sprigs parsley*

Blend the carrot juice and parsley together in a liquidizer or blender. Drink twice daily to relieve the symptoms. 1 serving

# fluid retention

When your body retains excess fluid it can make you feel uncomfortable, puffy and heavy, particularly around the waist and in the feet and hands. This tends to happen to women in the days leading up to a period and is related to changes in hormone levels causing a rise in the body's sodium levels. Chronic fluid retention can be caused by more serious problems including kidney and heart conditions which require professional treatment. In undernourished people, it can also be related to deficiencies of protein, vitamins and minerals.

To minimize fluid retention it is best to cut down on the amount of salt you eat, so avoid salty foods such as crisps, olives, anchovies, pickles, and smoked and cured meats like ham and bacon. This is not a good idea, however, if you live in or visit a hot country, if you are pregnant, or you take regular vigorous exercise which causes you to sweat a lot, as it could upset your fluid balance. The relationship between sodium and potassium in the body is such that the more potassium you take in the more you excrete sodium, so high potassium drinks, containing for example bananas and other fresh fruits, tomatoes and green vegetables, are a good idea.

It is important to drink at least 2-3 litres (4-6 pints) of fluid every day despite the tendency to suppose the opposite and restrict fluid intake. The more you drink the more you dilute the sodium in your body and the more you pass out through urination. Herbal teas, fruit and vegetable juices, and water are preferable in this instance to tea and coffee. Despite the fact that they have a diuretic action, tea and coffee actually encourage sodium retention and upset women's hormonal balance, only serving in the long run to aggravate the problem. There are plenty of potassium-rich fruits and vegetables with diuretic properties to provide a wealth of raw ingredients for alternative drinks – apples, cherries, blackcurrants, peaches and pears, carrots, cucumber, asparagus, celery, parsley, onions and turnips to name but a few.

## french potassium juice

The virtues of watercress have been sung for centuries and perhaps none louder than by the French who called it simply "*santé du corps*" meaning health of the body. Its wonderful peppery taste blends very well with the aromatic celery and parsley and the whole concoction produces an effective diuretic, abundant in potassium and a whole host of other nutrients to cleanse and nourish the system.

*1 bunch watercress, washed*
*3 large carrots, washed and cubed*
*3 large sticks celery, washed and chopped*
*6 sprigs parsley*

Juice the watercress, carrots and celery and then stir together. Serve with a garnish of chopped parsley. 1 serving

## scottish neep soup

The Scots are fond of this most ancient of vegetables, the turnip, which they call by its old-fashioned name, neep. It has been cultivated for about 3,000 years and has been recognized as an effective diuretic since at least Roman times. This thick, nutrition-packed soup, rich in vitamins and minerals including plenty of potassium, is enlivened by the aromatic thyme which adds its own diuretic properties.

*1 tablespoon olive oil*
*2 onions, peeled and sliced*
*175g (6oz) potatoes, peeled and diced*
*225g (8oz) small turnips, peeled and diced*
*1.2 litres (2 pints) vegetable or chicken stock*
*a few sprigs of thyme tied together in a bunch*
*salt and freshly ground pepper*
*a pinch of cayenne*
*chopped fresh parsley, to garnish*

Heat the oil in a large pan, add the onion and cook gently for 5 minutes. Add the potato, turnip, stock, thyme and seasoning. Bring to the boil, cover and simmer on a low heat for 20 minutes, until the vegetables are soft. Remove the thyme. Blend and adjust the seasoning. Garnish with a pinch of cayenne and some parsley and serve. 4 servings

## chinese waterfall

This sweet refreshing fruit juice tastes good enough to deserve a place on the menu in paradise and combines three ingredients which are valued by the Chinese for their cleansing and diuretic properties. Grapes, pears and melon are all highly nutritious, rich in vitamins and minerals including potassium, and they all strengthen and support the action of the kidneys. Try apple juice instead of grape juice, if you like.

*250ml (8fl oz) grape juice*
*250ml (8fl oz) pear juice*
*250ml (8fl oz) melon juice*
*ice cubes (optional)*
*ground ginger, to garnish*

Stir the fruit juices together well. Serve over ice if you wish with a little ginger sprinkled over the top. 2 servings

# 4

drinks for healing the soul and spirit

# drinks for healing the soul and spirit

While you might be surprised at the extent to which the common foodstuffs from our kitchens can benefit the health of our bodies, you may be even more amazed to know that they also have the power to influence the state of our minds and our emotions. Take depression, for example. Within our brains there are chemicals which help to transmit messages from one nerve cell to another. Two such chemicals that have a significant effect upon our mood, known as serotonin and noradrenaline, are made from the things we eat and drink. If our levels of these substances are low, we may have a tendency to feel low-spirited or depressed, and this can be reversed by eating specific foods. Sweet and high-carbohydrate foods are mood-elevating. Dried fruits, such as apricots, bananas, figs and dates, and whole grains like wheat, barley and oats can be made into drinks that can give you natural highs! Serotonin and noradrenaline are also made from amino acids found in certain protein foods, including fish and poultry, nuts and seeds.

Foods can also work in a more general way by supplying nutrition to support the work of the nervous system. Fruits and vegetables that are rich in vitamin C will help to protect us against the effects of stress. B vitamins are vital for our nerves and by including whole grains, nuts and seeds, green vegetables – broccoli, spinach, cabbage and asparagus – and milk in our drinks we will be helping to keep our mood stable. Green vegetables, nuts and seeds, oats, milk products and dried fruits are rich in minerals that are essential for the nervous system, particularly calcium and magnesium.

Some foods we choose because they harmonize our soul and spirit with the changing cycle of the seasons – hence we drink winter warmers and summer coolers, autumn boosters and spring renewals. Others are particularly comforting when we feel in need of a little tender loving care. Often the foods we choose to make us feel better have childhood connections with love and nurture. Perhaps this is the reason why we sometimes reach for sweet foods to comfort us; sweets are traditionally given to children as treats and rewards and, of course, breast milk, too, is sweet. According to Ayurveda, sweet foods increase *kapha* and induce a feeling of inner security and calm.

The addition of herbs and spices to our drinks to support us emotionally is the icing on the cake. Several of these such as lemon balm, St John's Wort and rosemary have the ability to lift the spirits and restore our *joie de vivre*. Others like lavender, chamomile, catmint, limeflower and vervain can calm our anxiety and allow restful sleep. Warming spices like cinnamon, ginger and cardamom are not only delicious in winter warming drinks but increase our energy and our ability to confront problems in our lives. Some herbs, including ginseng and licorice, can almost miraculously enhance our resilience to the stresses we encounter and help us to maintain our equilibrium almost against all odds. So while the drinks to follow will, hopefully, delight your taste buds, perhaps they will also reach your inner parts to give you nourishment and support in your daily life.

# relieving anxiety

Anxiety can be a perfectly normal response to a worrying situation such as an exam, a job interview or public speaking. It is short term and usually disappears easily once the event is over. Sometimes, however, worrying situations do not resolve themselves so easily. Ongoing difficulties between marital or work partners, worry about errant teenagers and financial problems, for example, can produce more long-term anxiety and our ability to cope with this will be challenged. Some people are clearly more able to deal with stress in their lives than others, some even suffer from a generalized feeling of anxiety for no particular reason. In susceptible people stress can trigger other problems such as digestive symptoms, insomnia, skin conditions, hormonal imbalances, panic attacks and heart palpitations.

There are many ways in which you can help yourself to cope better with stress and lower anxiety levels (see also Relieving Stress, p.138). Some time for reflection may allow you to see the underlying causes of your anxiety and suggest what changes you can make in your life to ease the situation. Plenty of exercise in one form or another and some deep breathing will disperse high adrenaline levels and help you to feel more relaxed. You may find yoga, *Tai chi,* relaxation exercises or meditation particularly helpful. It is always best to avoid caffeine-containing drinks as caffeine increases the effect of adrenaline and will increase your anxiety. Both caffeine and alcohol can disrupt sleep patterns, making you feel worse.

Drinks containing grounding and calming foods such as nuts and seeds, grains like oats and barley, vegetables such as lettuce, turnips and potatoes and sweet fruits like dates and bananas all help to relieve anxiety. In addition herbs and spices with relaxing effects are ideal. Lemon balm, rosemary, passionflower, chamomile, valerian, lavender, cloves and cardamom can be added to soups and juices or prepared as tisanes to be taken regularly until you feel better.

## provence lavender and lemon balm tisane

The lavender from Provence in France is famous for its magnificent aroma and flavour. Combined with lemon balm in this recipe it makes an exquisitely refreshing tea that tastes good enough for even the faint-hearted to enjoy. Lavender has a wonderfully relaxing effect on both mind and body and is excellent for reducing anxiety and stress-related symptoms such as headaches, insomnia and palpitations. Similarly, lemon balm has a naturally sedative effect, enhancing relaxation and inducing sleep.

*2 teaspoons lavender flowers*
*2 teaspoons lemon balm leaves*
*600ml (1 pint) boiling water*
*honey to taste (optional)*

Place the herbs in a teapot and pour over boiling water. Cover and leave to infuse for 10-15 minutes. Drink a cupful 3 times daily, or more if required. Sweeten with honey if you like. 2-3 servings

## italian potato, tomato and basil soup

My favourite of all soup recipes, this blend of potato, tomato and basil tastes like the epitomy of perfection. The nutritious potato provides valuable nutrients to support the nervous system such as B vitamins, vitamin C and potassium; the tomatoes provide vitamins A and E and plenty of iron. The basil that really makes this dish is a natural tranquillizer, relaxing tense muscles throughout the body and calming anxiety. It makes a wonderful remedy for all stress-related symptoms.

*4 tablespoons olive oil*
*1 large onion, peeled and sliced*
*1 bay leaf*
*1kg (2¼lb) potatoes, peeled and chopped roughly*
*salt and freshly ground pepper*
*1.5 litres (2½ pints) water*
*450g (1lb) tomatoes, skinned and chopped*
*2 handfuls of fresh basil leaves*

Heat 1 tablespoon of oil in a large pan. Add the onion and bay leaf and cook over medium heat for 4-5 minutes. Add the potatoes and a little salt, cover and cook over low heat for 5 minutes. Add the water, bring to the boil and simmer, covered, for about 20 minutes, until the potatoes are soft. Without draining, mash loosely with a potato masher; do not blend.

   Warm 1 tablespoon of oil in a pan. Add the tomatoes and cook over a medium heat until the mixture starts to thicken. Break up the tomatoes to form a sauce-like consistency. Season to taste and stir into the potato mixture. Combine the basil with 2 tablespoons of oil in a blender and season with salt and pepper. Serve with a spoonful of basil purée swirled into each bowl and plenty of freshly ground black pepper. 6 servings

# spring renewals

In nature spring is a time of new life and regeneration, and similarly for us it is a time to wake up and throw off the lethargy of winter. Drinks for spring need to be able to renew our energy and vitality and at the same time detoxify the body of toxins accumulated from the sedentary habits of the winter months. Certain foods and herbs such as watercress, dandelion leaves, young nettle tops, cabbage and leeks have the remarkable ability to do just this.

## tuscan spring tonic

*Ever since the 17th century celery has been popular with the Italians. In fact, the old French name for celery is* sceleri d'Italie. *Wonderfully aromatic, celery blends well with the rather similar taste of parsley, the pungency of garlic and the sweetness of carrot, to make this thick, highly nutritious vegetable juice. Perfect as a spring cleanser, celery, parsley and carrots all have diuretic properties, aiding the elimination of toxins via the kidneys, while garlic invigorates the whole body, disinfecting and cleansing as it goes.*

> 250ml (8fl oz) carrot juice
> 125ml (4fl oz) celery juice
> 1 garlic clove
> 1 handful of fresh parsley
> a few sprigs of parsley, to garnish

Blend all the ingredients together in a liquidizer or food processor. Serve with a garnish of parsley. 1 serving

## welsh dandelion beer

*This traditional Welsh recipe makes a beer that is excellent for quenching thirst and not very alcoholic. The combination of the bitterness of dandelions and the pungency of ginger is perfect for our purposes in spring. The bitter taste stimulates the function of the liver, the great detoxifying organ of the body, while the ginger's pungency has the effect of revitalizing the whole system, improving digestion and absorption while ensuring the removal of toxins and wastes.*

> 225g (8oz) young dandelion plants
> 4.5 litres (8 pints) water
> 15g (½oz) root ginger, sliced and
>   bruised
> finely peeled rind and juice of
>   1 lemon
> 450g (1lb) demerara sugar
> 25g (1oz) cream of tartar
> 7g (¼oz) dried brewer's yeast

Dig up complete young dandelion plants, wash them well and remove all the fibrous roots, leaving the main tap root. Place in a large saucepan with the water, ginger and lemon rind. Bring to the boil and simmer for 10 minutes. Strain and pour on to the sugar and cream of tartar in a fermentation bucket. Stir until the sugar has dissolved. Start the yeast following the instructions and add it to the lukewarm must with the lemon juice. Cover and leave in a warm room for 3 days. Strain into screw-top bottles. It will be ready to drink after 1 week and, if stored in a cool place, will keep for about a month.

## nettle and cabbage soup

*The abundant chlorophyll in nettles gives this soup a wonderfully vibrant colour that makes you feel healthy just looking at it. Bursting with vitamins, minerals and trace elements, it nourishes and cleanses at the same time. An antiseptic, a diuretic, a tonic to the liver and a laxative, cabbage makes an ideal spring tonic, explaining its ancient reputation for purifying the blood. Similarly, nettles stimulate the liver and kidneys, cleansing the body of toxins and wastes, and restore vitality to the system.*

*1 tablespoon olive oil*
*1 large onion, peeled and chopped*
*2 leeks, washed and sliced*
*100g (4oz) cabbage, chopped*
*1.2 litres (2 pints) vegetable or*
*  chicken stock*
*salt and freshly ground pepper*
*2 handfuls nettle tops, washed*
*2 tablespoons chopped fresh*
*  parsley or coriander*
*ground nutmeg, to garnish*

Heat the oil in a saucepan, add the onion and cook until soft. Add the leeks and cabbage, cover and cook on a low heat for 10 minutes. Add the stock and seasoning. Bring to the boil and simmer for 20 minutes, adding the nettles for the last few minutes. Remove from the heat and blend. Add the parsley or coriander before serving and garnish with nutmeg. 4 servings

# calming a restless mind

When stress or anxiety weigh heavily upon us and interfere with our ability to relax and reflect, we can look to the world of plants to help restore some balance and harmony. Simply spending time in the garden or going for a walk in the countryside can calm the mind. If you are having trouble mentally switching off, try drinking calming herbal teas such as chamomile, limeflower, mint, lemon balm or catmint. These are ideal for relieving tense muscles and slowing down an overactive mind, both of which can hinder peaceful contemplation and meditation, or interfere with normal concentration at work.

Oats, wheat, barley and rice have a grounding and calming effect on the body and mind, as do almonds, bananas and dates. If eaten with mild spices, such as cardamom and cinnamon, these ingredients can help induce a peaceful, meditative state. Interestingly, oats and spices also play a part in helping us to raise our energy (see p. 56). If you're suffering from stress or restlessness, avoid stimulating drinks such as coffee or tea.

## banana calmer

This smooth, creamy and comforting banana milk shake will help to soothe your mind. The high starch content and nutritious qualities of bananas may be wonderfully grounding when you are burning up lots of nervous energy. With its mild soothing effect, this sweet drink is excellent for calming your restlessness, especially if it's caused by overwork and stress.

*250ml (8fl oz) milk*
*1 banana, peeled and sliced*
*4 ice cubes*
*1 tablespoon honey*
*a pinch of ground or freshly grated nutmeg*

Blend all the ingredients in a liquidizer or food processor until smooth. Serve sprinkled with extra nutmeg if desired. 1 serving

## greek lettuce soup

This delicious, cold soup is ideal for calming you down on hot flustery days. The cooling effects of the yogurt and lettuce can help you slow down on days when your mind will not rest. The mint garnish helps to stimulate blood flow to the head, clearing the mind.

1 tablespoon olive oil
2 medium onions, peeled and sliced
2 potatoes, peeled and diced
1 garlic clove, crushed
1 large lettuce, chopped
900ml (1½ pint) chicken or vegetable stock
salt and freshly ground pepper
3 tablespoons thick natural yogurt
freshly chopped mint leaves, to garnish

Heat the oil in a saucepan and gently fry the onions, potatoes and garlic for 5 minutes. Add the lettuce, stock and seasoning. Bring to the boil, cover and simmer over low heat until the vegetables are tender. Leave the soup to cool for a short time. Blend in a liquidizer then stir in the yogurt. Chill in the refrigerator for 3-4 hours. Serve garnished with mint. 4 servings

## serenity smoothie

A deliciously sweet drink that will nourish and settle your mind. The sweetness of the rice milk, almonds and dates is offset by the spicy flavour of the ginger that brings in more than a hint of the East. All the ingredients have a strengthening and stabilizing effect on the nerves, helping to improve memory and concentration – no wonder these foods have been popular for bringing peace of mind in India for thousands of years.

1 tablespoon ground almonds
100g (4oz) dates (stones removed)
350ml (12fl oz) water or rice milk
1 teaspoon ground ginger

Blend all the ingredients together in a liquidizer or food processor until smooth. 1 serving

## summer coolers

The idea of bliss on a hot summer's afternoon is to relax in a hammock or a chair in the shade of a lovely old fruit tree in the garden and idly while away the hours doing nothing more than lazily sipping a cooling fruity drink from time to time. There are certain foods and herbs that make perfect summer drinks including cucumber, watercress, bananas, melon, mangoes, elderflowers, mint, lemon balm and yogurt. Not only do they taste delightful in cold drinks, but they also have cooling properties themselves.

### mintade

*No other herb can rival the refreshing taste of fresh mint leaves in summer and when combined with lemon and ice they make an ideal drink for when you are hot and thirsty. Interestingly, in the language of flowers, mint represents eternal refreshment. The cooling effect of mint is experienced on the tongue the minute it is tasted, and this soon disperses throughout the rest of the body. Its ability to revive mind and body is particularly welcome after a heavy lunch when lethargy on a hot afternoon threatens to overcome our efficiency at work.*

1½ lemons, washed
2 tablespoons fresh mint leaves, crushed
1½ tablespoons sugar
600ml (1 pint) boiling water
ice cubes
a few sprigs of mint, to garnish

Slice the lemons, saving the juice. Place in a jug with the mint and sugar. Pour on boiling water and leave to steep for 2 hours. Strain and serve in glasses over ice, garnished with sprigs of mint. 2-3 servings

### english elderflower cordial

*This delicately scented cordial makes a light, fruity tasting and wonderfully refreshing drink. One sip and immediately you are transported to the perfection of a warm summer's afternoon in the beauty of England's countryside. The cooling effect of elderflowers is brought about in two main ways. By bringing blood to the surface of the body, heat is released through the pores of the skin, and by their diuretic action, excess heat as well as toxins are eliminated via the kidneys.*

1.2 litres (2 pints) water
1.3 kg (3lb) sugar
1 lemon, sliced
25 large elderflower heads
75g (3oz) citric acid
sparkling or still mineral water to dilute

Place the water in a large pan and bring to the boil. Add the sugar and lemon and remove from the heat until the sugar dissolves. Place on the heat again and bring to the boil. Add the elderflower heads and citric acid. Bring to the boil once more, remove from the heat and allow to stand until cool. Strain and bottle in clean bottles with corks. This can be drunk immediately. Stored in a cool place it should keep approximately 3 months. When serving, dilute with 5 parts water and add ice.

## cold cucumber and mint soup

*The cooling, thirst-quenching cucumber is a perfect partner for mint, the most refreshing of herbs. Together they make an exquisite tasting cold soup for a hot day, the mild pungency of the mint and spring onions contrasting with the blandness of the cucumber. The yogurt gives it a lovely creamy consistency and additional cooling properties.*

*1 large cucumber, peeled and diced*
*6 spring onions, trimmed and chopped*
*250ml (8fl oz) water (or vegetable or chicken stock)*
*3 tablespoons Greek natural yogurt*
*juice of 1 lemon*
*6 sprigs fresh mint*
*salt and freshly ground pepper*

Blend the cucumber, spring onions and water (or stock) together until smooth. Add the yogurt and lemon juice. Strip the mint leaves from the stems, reserving a few to garnish, then finely chop and stir into the yogurt mixture. Season to taste. Cover and refrigerate for 1 hour. Garnish with mint when serving. 3-4 servings

# relieving stress

Stress is a natural and unavoidable facet of life. Although most of us tend to view it as entirely negative, it can be a great motivator, providing it does not get out of hand. It is often said that stress is not in itself a problem, it's how you respond to it. Clearly people's reaction to stress varies according to their constitutions and temperaments. Some are easy-going and do not easily become stressed while others are more sensitive and vulnerable. What is important is to find the right balance between stress and relaxation. Prolonged stress will gradually deplete our vital energy and lead to exhaustion and illness, for some of us faster than others.

You should always eat a good diet regularly and sleep well. Vitamins B and C and minerals zinc, potassium, calcium, magnesium and iron are considered the most important nutrients in the battle against stress. You need to eat plenty of whole grains, nuts and seeds, fruit and vegetables to provide you with these, while a diet high in sugar, refined carbohydrates and junk foods can contribute to deficiencies.

Foods such as bananas, dates, figs, almonds, cashews, coconut, avocado, mango and papaya all have a calming and strengthening effect on the nerves. Spices including cardamom, cinnamon, ginger, coriander and cloves are great relievers of stress. Several herbs have a marvellously strengthening effect upon the nervous system – ginseng, licorice, skullcap, vervain, wood betony and lemon balm are good examples. Other herbs, such as lavender, rosemary, chamomile, basil, motherwort, hops, licorice, limeflower and passionflower, can safely be used instead of orthodox tranquillizers if you are feeling tense or have trouble sleeping. They are completely nonaddictive.

## tanzanian banana and coconut milk

Many recipes in Tanzania, including soups, stews and desserts, are based on bananas and plantain and often combined with coconut. The mixture of the two sweet tastes in this recipe is wonderful. Both bananas and coconut are highly nutritious, rich in B vitamins, calcium, magnesium, iron and potassium. They are strengthening, even rejuvenating and with their grounding and calming effect are ideal foods for relieving stress.

*3 medium-sized, ripe bananas*
*250ml (8fl oz) coconut milk*
*a little ground cinnamon*

Place the bananas and coconut milk in a liquidizer and blend until smooth. Sprinkle cinnamon on the top when serving.  **1-2 servings**

## middle eastern avocado soup

In countries like Turkey and Israel they are very fond of chilled avocado soup which is often served as a main dish in the summer. It is thick and creamy and in this recipe the blandness of the avocado is offset by the pungency of the ginger. Avocados are rich in nutrients for the nervous system, including vitamins B and C, potassium and iron. They calm and strengthen the nerves and are excellent during times of stress.

*3 large avocados, peeled and chopped*
*500ml (16fl oz) vegetable or chicken stock*
*juice of 1½ lemons*
*6 spring onions, chopped*
*3 garlic cloves, peeled*
*250ml (8fl oz) crème fraîche or natural yogurt*
*1-2.5cm (½-1in) piece fresh root ginger,*
*  peeled and grated*
*salt and freshly ground pepper*
*fresh parsley, to garnish*

Place the avocado in a blender with the stock and lemon juice and blend until smooth. Add the spring onions, garlic, crème fraîche (or yogurt) and ginger to taste, then blend again. Season with salt and pepper. Cover and chill for 1 hour. Add more stock, if too thick, and lemon juice to taste. Serve garnished with parsley. 4 servings

# autumn boosters

The "season of mists and mellow fruitfulness" is certainly a good time to make use of the abundant fruit that might otherwise go to waste on the ground in the orchard or in the fruit bowl. Drinks packed with vitamins and minerals made from apples, pears, plums, blackberries and elderberries, provide vital nutrients for the immune system and serve to prepare us well for the onslaught of winter and the ills it may bring. Spices added to enhance the flavour of the fruit have the extra benefit of stimulating the circulation, keeping us warm as the weather turns colder.

## elderberry rob

*This rich dark-red cordial is a storehouse of vitamins A and C, and a delicious syrupy remedy for preventing and treating coughs, colds and flu, sore throats and fevers. Until the end of the 19th century hot elderberry drinks were sold on the streets of London on cold winter days and nights to give cheer to workers and travellers and to keep out the cold. Cinnamon was often added to elderberry rob to enhance its warming effect.*

*450g (1lb) fresh elderberries*
*450g (1lb) brown sugar*

Strip the berries from their stems, wash and then crush them. Place in a pan with the sugar. Bring slowly to the boil and simmer until a syrupy consistency is reached. Pass through a sieve and bottle in clean, airtight bottles. Take 1-2 tablespoons in a cup of hot water regularly as a preventative or at the onset of cold symptoms. This recipe works well with other fruit such as blackberries and blackcurrants.

## italian tomato juice

*The bright red "love apple" as the tomato used to be called, always looks inviting in drinks and this thick, piquant juice is no exception. Tomatoes have been popular in Italian cuisine ever since the Middle Ages when a Fra Serenio brought the precious seeds back from his travels in China. Rich in antioxidant vitamins and minerals, they boost energy and vitality, aid the elimination of toxins and enhance the body's fight against infection.*

*450g (1lb) ripe tomatoes, chopped*
*2 teaspoons lemon juice*
*3 teaspoons Worcestershire sauce*
*1 teaspoon soy sauce*
*salt to taste*
*a pinch of cayenne pepper*
*fresh or dried thyme, to garnish*

Blend together the tomatoes, lemon juice, Worcestershire sauce, soy sauce, salt and cayenne pepper in a liquidizer or food processor. Strain and serve over ice and with a garnish of thyme.  3-4 servings

## french apple and cinnamon tea

*The traditional combination of apple and cinnamon works well in this sweet and spicy tea. The tart flavour and cold properties of the apples are balanced by the sweetness and warming properties of the honey and cinnamon. Jean Valnet, the French phyto-therapist, recommends apple tea to be taken daily to prevent cold and flu viruses and to ward off arthritis and gout.*

4 apples, washed and sliced
600ml (1 pint) water
2 tablespoons honey
1 teaspoon ground cinnamon

Place the apples in a pan, add the water, cover and cook on a low heat until soft. Strain then stir in the honey and cinnamon. Serve hot. 2-3 servings

# healing emotions

It is inevitable that emotional upheavals will weave themselves into the tapestries of our lives and in many instances they will serve as our teachers and give us insight into what it really means to be human. For this reason it is not always advisable to try to rid ourselves of uncomfortable and painful emotions by using orthodox drugs, for example, to sedate us, to stop depression or mask the pain.

What we do always need in difficult times in our lives is support. We need friends or family for a shoulder to cry on, for talking things through and a chance to express our emotions. However, we can also use foods and herbs to support and heal us as we work through our problems, so that the stress they impose does not lead to nervous exhaustion and physical illness.

To enhance our resilience in a general way to the stress that emotional problems impose on our nervous systems we need to support the body and specifically the nerves (see Relieving Stress, p. 138). For our emotions themselves the almost miraculous world of flowers offers a wealth of healing, for flowers seem to have the power to heal us on all levels of our being. They can act as catalysts to self awareness and understanding, to releasing emotional blocks and allowing us to let go of pain that results from broken relationships, grief and trauma.

Pasque flower, for example, is the perfect remedy for those feeling insecure, tearful, lonely and vulnerable with a fear of being forsaken. Hyssop makes a wonderful nerve tonic to relieve anxiety, tension, exhaustion and depression that have their origin in emotional problems and specifically with feelings of guilt. Hyssop helps us to let go of such feelings and allow self forgiveness.

## indian rose syrup and coconut milk

Just tasting this sweet nectar is enough to bring joy to the heart. Roses have long been associated with love and all affairs of the heart. They have a wonderfully uplifting and restorative effect and can be thought of whenever you feel tense, anxious, depressed, angry, lonely and upset. They are specifically for those who lack love in their lives. In India coconut is seen as a gift from the gods to human beings and a token of good luck in romantic relationships.

*1 tablespoon rose syrup*
*250ml (8fl oz) coconut milk*
*ice cubes*

To make rose syrup collect rose petals, weigh them and place in a bowl with an equal weight of sugar. Mash the petals and sugar together, cover and leave overnight. Strain through a fine sieve, pour into clean bottles and store in the refrigerator. Stir a tablespoonful of syrup into a cup of coconut milk. Add ice and dilute with a little water, if required. The syrup will keep for about a month. 1 serving

## english heartsease and chamomile infusion

Wild pansy or heartease derives its name from its ability to heal the heart, to soothe the pain of separation from loved ones and to ease a broken heart. Chamomile also helps to ease emotional pain, to soothe anger and conflict and to release tension accumulating from inner problems that might otherwise contribute to stress-related illness and insomnia. The combination of the two makes a pleasant light tisane, perfect for promoting inner harmony.

*½ teaspoon heartease flowers*
*½ teaspoon chamomile flowers*
*250ml (8fl oz) boiling water*
*honey to taste (optional)*

Place the herbs in a small teapot and pour over boiling water. Cover and leave to infuse for 10-15 minutes before serving. Sweeten with honey if you like. 1 serving

## borage and lemon balm fruit cup

Borage flowers and lemon balm leaves floated in fruit juices, such as apple or pear, make delightfully refreshing drinks for a hot summer's day that can, at the same time, help to ease emotional pain. Borage has a generally relaxing effect and is famous for its ability to dispel grief and sadness and to aid the heavy-hearted, broken-hearted or down-hearted. Lemon balm lifts the spirits, balances the emotions and imparts inner strength and courage.

*600ml (1 pint) apple or pear juice*
*1 handful fresh borage flowers*
*1 handful fresh lemon balm leaves*

Heat the fruit juice in a pan until almost boiling. Place 1 teaspoon of each of the herbs in a jug and pour over the hot fruit juice. Cover and leave to cool. Strain into a clean jug and float a few borage flowers and lemon balm leaves to decorate. Serve with ice if desired. 2-3 servings

# winter warmers

Fruit, vegetables, herbs and spices provide many warming remedies that stimulate the circulation of blood around the body and dilate the blood vessels so that warmth reaches even to those cold extremities. You only have to taste some of these remedies and experience the burning sensation on the tongue and then that warm feeling in the stomach, to know that ginger, garlic, onions, leeks and cayenne are just the thing for a cold winter's day.

## caribbean lime and cayenne syrup

*Cayenne is a major stimulant to the heart and circulation, perfect for warming chilly people and for warding off "blues" and lethargy.*

*600ml (1 pint) water*
*1.3kg (3lb) sugar*
*1 egg white*
*600ml (1 pint) lime juice*
*1-2 teaspoons cayenne pepper, to taste*

Whisk the water, sugar and egg white together in a saucepan. Bring to the boil and simmer slowly for 10 minutes. Add the lime juice and simmer for a further minute. Add the cayenne, stir and leave to cool. Bottle and seal well. Take two tablespoons in a cup of hot water when required.

## szechwan soup

*The combination of the onions, garlic and ginger of this centuries-old hot and sour Chinese soup has a power-fully stimulating effect, increasing blood flow throughout the body and dispelling winter cold most effectively.*

*5 dried Chinese mushrooms (or any mushroom of your choice)*
*25g (1oz) rice noodles*
*1.5 litres (2½ pints) chicken stock*
*100g (4oz) chopped cooked chicken*
*225g (8oz) bamboo shoots, tinned, drained*
*2 teaspoons freshly grated root ginger*
*2 garlic cloves, finely chopped*
*1 egg, beaten*
*½ tablespoon tomato purée*
*1 tablespoon soy sauce*
*1 tablespoon cider vinegar*
*2 teaspoons sesame oil*
*3 spring onions, finely chopped*
*salt and freshly ground pepper*

Soak the Chinese mushrooms in hot water in a bowl for 30 minutes, then drain and chop. Soak the noodles in cold water for 20 minutes, drain and cut into short lengths. Heat the chicken stock in a large pan and bring to the boil. Add the mushrooms, chicken, bamboo shoots, ginger, garlic and noodles. Reduce the heat, cover and simmer gently for 4 minutes, then add the egg in a fine stream, stirring all the time. Remove the pan from the heat and add the remaining ingredients, reserving a few spring onions to garnish. Season with salt and pepper and serve topped with spring onions. 4 servings

## medieval ginger cordial

*Truly invigorating and spicy, this cordial has been a traditional favourite in monasteries since the Dark Ages. It stimulates the heart and circulation, making you feel warm right down to your toes.*

*100g (4oz) dried figs*
*¼ teaspoon ground allspice*
*a few slices of fresh root ginger*
*¼ teaspoon ground nutmeg*
*1 cinnamon stick*
*4 cloves*
*600ml (1 pint) ginger beer*
*1 teaspoon lemon juice*

Stew the figs in enough water to cover them, until soft, then blend to a smooth paste. Return to the pan, add the spices and ginger beer, and heat slowly, then simmer, covered, for 10 minutes. Add the lemon juice. Strain and drink a cupful hot when required. 2-3 servings

# helping depression

There are many ways to maintain and restore balance and harmony in your life so that you feel good again, without masking warning symptoms perhaps designed to initiate change. Foods, herbs and spices can all play their part in nurturing the nervous system and many of them have specifically mood-elevating properties that help to dispel negativity and lift the spirits.

Many of us feel tired, low, or lacking in enthusiasm, inspiration, even interest, from time to time. This often occurs in winter and particularly affects people who tend to feel cold and lethargic in cold weather. Foods with a cold quality, such as dairy products, sugar and wheat products, are best reduced to a minimum in these instances, while warming spices – ginger, cardamom, cloves and cinnamon – are just the thing to lift the spirits. By increasing the circulation and thereby the efficiency of every cell in the body, these spices increase energy and impart a sense of wellbeing.

Certain foodstuffs can lift the spirits by raising endorphin levels. Dried fruits, such as dates, figs and apricots, and carbohydrates like rice, as well as honey, all increase these mood-enhancing endorphins. Proteins such as almonds and sesame seeds are also excellent ingredients for drinks to dispel the blues.

Black pepper, with its pungent taste and warming properties, is also excellent for warding off lethargy. Its stimulating properties help to dispel nervous debility, low spirits and depression and will have you feeling cheerful whatever the weather. Cardamom serves as a great energy tonic, helping to generate strength, lift the spirits and allay lethargy and depression. Used extensively in the Far East, Middle East, Europe and Latin America for flavouring drinks, particularly liqueurs and medicines, cardamom makes a tasty addition to hot punches, spiced wines and teas, too.

## lemon balm tea

A wonderful remedy for the nerves, lemon balm restores energy and lifts low spirits as well as calming tension and anxiety.

*25g (1oz) fresh lemon balm leaves*
*600ml (1 pint) boiling water*

Place the lemon balm in a teapot and pour over boiling water. Put the lid on and leave to infuse for 10-15 minutes. Drink, hot or cold, up to four times a day. 2-3 servings

## carob inspiration

The carob bean is delicious in warm drinks, bringing a hint of Mediterranean sunshine to a gloomy day. It is naturally sweet and energy-giving, a wonderfully comforting and grounding drink. Cardamom and milk are an excellent combination as cardamoms have the ability to dispel the mucus-forming properties of milk. When making this recipe, it is important not to boil the cardamoms.

*600ml (1 pint) milk or soya milk*
*4 teaspoons carob powder*
*5 cardamom pods, crushed*
*honey to taste*

Add 1 tablespoonful of milk to the carob powder and stir into a smooth paste. Heat the rest of the milk in a pan, add the cardamom pods, then cover and keep almost at simmering point for 20 30 minutes. Strain the milk, return to the pan and add the carob paste. Stir and heat gently for a further 2 minutes. Remove from the heat. 2-3 servings

## mood-lifting tea

Cardamom is not only a delicious spice but also an energy tonic and restorative to warm and inspire. Cardamom comes from India, where it has long been used in Ayurvedic medicine to lift the spirits, dispel cold and depression, restore strength and vitality, and to induce a calm, meditative state of mind.

*600ml (1 pint) cold water*
*4 black peppercorns*
*4 cardamom pods*
*1 cinnamon stick*
*4 cloves*
*a few slices of fresh root ginger*
*milk and/or honey to taste*

Place the water and spices in a pan and heat to nearly boiling (never boil). Cover and simmer for an hour. Strain and serve. Add a little milk and/or honey if you like. Drink a cupful 2-3 times daily. 2-3 servings

# appendix

## equipment

All the drinks in this book are very quick and easy to make providing you have a few basic pieces of equipment. The most basic equipment of all is, of course, your two hands and some bowls or jugs, and they will very often prove quite adequate. However, a simple piece of machinery very often will do in a few seconds what it would take your hands a lot longer to accomplish.

### Blenders, liquidizers and food processors

These machines can be used interchangeably and are designed to blend all parts of a variety of ingredients together until even-textured and smooth. In smooth soups, for example, the ingredients are cooked as instructed in the recipe then, before serving, are blended by high-speed shredding. The process transforms the mixture of chunky vegetables in liquid into a homogenous consistency.

Fruit drinks and smoothies prepared in a blender, liquidizer or food processor have the advantage of retaining all their fibre, which is well known to be vital to the health of the bowel, as well as having the effect of reducing cholesterol levels.

If you do not possess a blender it is possible to blend to some degree by hand but it is a much lengthier process. When making a smoothie for example, you can mash the ripe fruit with a fork then blend it with the other ingredients in a bowl. The result will never be as smooth and creamy but it will be equally tasty and just as good for you. If you want to incorporate healthy drinks into your daily routine, however, it would be worth investing in a machine.

An electric hand blender is a good alternative if you are blending large quantities – when making soup, for example. If you use a liquidizer this can involve a lot of work, as you have to transfer the ingredients from the pan to the liquidizer to be blended in batches. It is often very much easier to insert a hand blender into the ingredients wherever they happen to be – in a bowl, a jug or a pan – and switch it on. Within a few minutes or even seconds the work is done.

### Juicers

Juicers are designed to extract the juice from fruits, vegetables and herbs while leaving the fibre behind, and there is a variety of different types available. Many of us have been juicing for years using a simple lemon squeezer to extract our citrus juices, and this still remains a good option for these purposes. Electric citrus juicers, which are based on the same principle, significantly reduce the amount of elbow power needed.

It is possible to extract juices from fruit and vegetables by hand but it is hard work. You grate the fruit or vegetable into a bowl, then place it in a piece of clean muslin and squeeze as hard as you can. The amount of juice extracted will depend on your strength and persistence!

The juices of some vegetables, onion and cabbage, for example, can be extracted using a covering of honey or sugar which have hydroscopic properties that draw the liquid out (see Nero's Nectar, p. 81; Cabbage and Coriander Syrup, p. 85).

To extract juices from other fruit and vegetables you really do need a juicer. There are several types of machine and the one you choose will depend on the kinds of ingredients you want to juice; how easy the machine is to take apart to wash and then reassemble; its size; and the price.

Centrifugal juicers, the least expensive, can cope with only small quantities of material at a time, but for most individual's purposes they serve quite adequately. Like the other types of machine they chop up the ingredients at high speed and then separate the juice from the pulp.

Masticating juicers are slightly more expensive but are more efficient as they cope better with hard bits of skin and pips.

Hydraulic juicers can cope with large quantities and extract more juice from the chopped-up pulp, but tend to cost the most. You get what you pay for.

### Cleaning equipment

Wash all the equipment you use thoroughly after use to avoid contaminating and spoiling drinks with lingering tastes from former preparations. If strong-tasting ingredients do linger you may find that putting apple or lemon through the machine will not only resolve this but also help to remove stains on your equipment.

# general advice

## Choosing ingredients

Whatever method you use to make your drinks, you should choose the best-quality ingredients you can; tired-looking fruits and vegetables are never going to match those freshly picked for either taste or goodness.

Use organic fruit and vegetables if they are available. As well as being free from the health risks associated with the use of pesticides, organic fruit and vegetables will often provide additional nutrients, since you do not usually need to peel them.

In order that nutrients (vitamins A and C and folic acid, in particular) that diminish during storage are not lost, it is a good idea to buy fresh ingredients in small quantities and use them quickly.

## Bought juices

It is always preferable to extract fruit and vegetable juices yourself, as freshly prepared drinks score highest in terms of maximum nutritional benefit. However, shop bought equivilants are well worth buying if you do not have the means to make your own. Look in health food shops for the more unusual juices, such as beetroot and cabbage.

## Frozen, dried and tinned foods

Fresh fruit and vegetables are best for all the recipes in this book, but if an ingredient is unavailable or out of season, frozen, dried or tinned versions will do.

Choose tinned fruit preserved in fruit juice or water, rather than in a heavy syrup, and sun-dried fruits, such as apricots, rather than sulphur-dried versions, which can cause allergic reactions in some sensitive people.

## Finishing touches

The garnishes used in the recipes – fruits, vegetables, herbs or spices – often enhance the medicinal benefits of the drinks. They also make your drinks look inviting, however, and add extra excitement to the taste.

The glasses or bowls in which you serve your drinks can add further to their presentation so that you produce drinks that not only taste wonderful and do you a power of good but look tempting as well.

## Drink as soon as possible

It is important to consume your drinks as soon as possible after preparing them so that the maximum nutrition remains. Certain nutrients (folic acid and vitamins A and C, for Instance), are not stable and will diminish on exposure to light and air, standing and storing.

Soups can be kept for a day or two but freshly extracted vegetable and fruit juices and smoothies are best consumed immediately, since most of the goodness is lost within 20 minutes.

## Juice fasting

Drinking only fruit and vegetable juices or water for a day (not more than once a week but recommended at least once a month) is excellent not only for cleansing the body thoroughly but also for invigorating body and mind. Juice fasting gives the whole digestive system a day off and is an excellent way to rid the body of toxins.

Grape juice is the most popular choice for juice fasts, whether drunk alone or with other juices. Look for recipes in the book that are detoxifying – ones that include grape, carrot, beetroot and apple, for example – or act as laxatives. Don't drink more than one glassful of pure carrot juice a day or more than four glassfuls a week.

**Note:** *Do not go on a juice fast if you are pregnant, if you suffer from anaemia or diabetes, or if you have an eating disorder. Consult your doctor if you are in doubt.*

## Making herbal teas

To prepare herbal tea you need either a teapot or a small pan and a sieve. Use about 2 teaspoonfuls of dried herb (or 4 teaspoonfuls of fresh) to 600ml (1 pint) water. You can vary the amount according to taste.

When using the soft parts of a herb, such as the flower, stems or leaves, place the correct amount of the herb in a warm teapot and pour over boiling water. Cover and leave to stand for 10 to 15 minutes to allow the hot water to extract the medicinal components from the plant. Use this method for basil, rosemary, thyme and lemon balm teas, for example.

When using the hard parts of a herb or spice – the seeds, bark or roots (cinnamon bark, coriander seed or ginger root, for example) – greater heat is required to extract the constituents. You will need to place them in a pan with cold water, bring to the boil, cover and simmer for 10 to 15 minutes. Strain and sweeten with honey if you like.

## Quantities

1 teaspoon (level) = 5ml
1 tablespoon (level) = 15ml
1 cupful or glassful = 250ml (8fl oz)
1 small glassful = 90ml (3fl oz)
1 large glassful = 350ml (12fl oz)

# useful terms

**Adaptogenic**  Helps to restore balance within the body

**Anaesthetic**  Deadens sensation and reduces pain

**Analgesic**  Pain relieving

**Antibacterial**  Destroys or stops the growth of bacterial infections

**Antibiotic**  Destroys or stops the growth of bacteria

**Antidiuretic**  Decreases urine production

**Antifungal**  Treats fungal infections

**Anti-inflammatory**  Reduces inflammation

**Antimicrobial**  Destroys or stops the growth of micro-organisms

**Antioxidant**  Prevents damage by free radicals and helps protects against degenerative disease

**Antiparasitical**  Kills parasites

**Antiseptic**  Prevents putrefaction

**Antispasmodic**  Prevents or relieves spasms or cramps

**Antiviral**  Destroys or stops the growth of viral infections

**Astringent**  Contracts tissue, drying and reducing secretions or discharges

**Bactericidal**  Able to destroy bacteria

**Decoction**  Herbal tea made from the hard parts of a plant, such as he seeds, bark or roots

**Decongestant**  Relieves congestion

**Detoxifying**  Eliminating toxins from the body

**Digestive**  Aids digestion

**Disinfectant**  Destroys or inhibits the activity of micro-organisms that cause disease

**Diuretic**  Promotes the flow of urine

**Endorphins**  Natural substances synthesized in the pineal gland which have an analgesic effect

**Expectorant**  Promotes expulsion of mucus from the repiratory tract

**Infusion**  Herbal tea made from the soft parts of a herb – the flower, stems or leaves

**Laxative**  Promotes evacuation of the bowels

**Panacea**  A remedy for all ills or disorders

**Relaxant**  Relaxes nerves and muscles

**Restorative**  Restores normal physiological activity and energy

**Stimulant**  Produces energy and increases circulation

**Tisane**  An infusion made from fresh or dried herbs

**Tonic**  Invigorates and tones the body and promotes wellbeing

# further reading

*The Around the World Cookbook*, Hermes House, UK, 1998

Ayto J., *Food & Drink from A to Z*, Oxford University Press, UK, 1994

Bareham L., *A Celebration of Soup*, Penguin Books Ltd, UK, 1994

Bigg, M., *Complete Book of Vegetables*, Kyle Cathie Ltd, UK, 1997

Black, M., *The Medieval Cookbook*, British Museum Press, UK, 1993

Bragg, G., and Simon, D., *The Ayurvedic Cookbook*, Rider & Co. Ltd, UK, 1997

Calbom, C., and Keane, M., *Juicing for Life*, Avery Publishing Inc, USA, 1992

Carper, J., *Miracle Cures*, Thorsons, UK, 1997

Chatto, J., and Martin, W., *A Kitchen in Corfu*, Weidenfeld & Nicolson, UK, 1993

Clarke, J., *Body Foods For Women*, Weidenfeld & Nicolson, UK, 1996

Conil, J., and Franklin, F., *Fabulous French Fruit Cuisine*, Thorsons, UK, 1988

Dalby, A., and Grainger, S., *The Classical Cookbook*, British Museum Press, UK, 1996

Ewin, J., *The Plants We Need To Eat*, Thorsons, UK, 1997

*Foods That Harm, Foods That Heal*, Reader's Digest, UK, 1996

Gee, M., and Goldin, G., *The Longevity Chinese Vegetarian Cookbook*, Thorsons, UK, 1987

Geelhoed, G., and Barilla, M., *Natural Health Secrets*, Keats Publishing, USA, 1997

Gentry, P., and Devereux, L., *Juice it Up!*, The Cole Group, USA, 1991

Giller, Dr. R., and Matthews, K., *Natural Prescriptions*, BCA/Pavillion Books, UK, 1995

Hafner, D., *A Taste of Africa*, Headline Book Publishing, UK, 1997

Hammond, P., *Food and Feast in Medieval England*, Alan Sutton Publishing, UK, 1993

Heinerman, J., *Heinerman's New Encyclopedia of Fruits & Vegetables*, Parker Publishing Co., USA, 1995

Honey, B., *Drinks for All Seasons*, EP Publishing Ltd, UK, 1982

Hurley, J., *The Good Herb*, William Morrow & Co., USA, 1995

Johari, H., *The Healing Cuisine*, Healing Arts Press, USA, 1994

Lad, V., and Frawley, D., *The Yoga of Herbs*, Lotus Press, USA, 1986

Laurence, S., *Feasting on Herbs*, Kyle Cathie Ltd, UK, 1995

Lousada, P., *Cooking with Herbs*, Bloomsbury Books, UK, 1994

Lukins, S., *All Around the World Cookbook*, Workman Publishing Co., USA, 1994

McIntyre, A., *The Good Health Garden*, Reader's Digest, UK, 1998

Paterson, W., *A Country Cup*, Pelham Books, UK, 1980

Patten, M., *Soups*, Bloomsbury Publishing Plc, UK, 1997

Polunin, M., *Healing Foods*, Dorling Kindersley, UK, 1997

Routh, S., and J., *Leonardo's Kitchen Note Books*, Collins, UK, 1987

Scott, D., *Middle Eastern Vegetarain Cookery*, Rider & Co. Ltd, UK, 1982

Scully, T., *The Art of Cookery in the Middle Ages*, Boydell Press, UK, 1995

Valnet, J., *Heal Yourself With Vegetables, Fruits and Grains*, Cornerstone Library, USA, 1976

Wadey, R., *Soups & Broths*, Paragon Book Service, UK, 1996

Wheater, C., *Juicing for Health*, Thorsons, UK, 1993

Whiteman, K., and Mayhew, M., *The World Encyclopedia of Fruit*, Lorenz Books, UK, 1998

Willis, J., *The Food Bible*, Quadrille Publishing Ltd, UK, 1998

# resources

## Fruit juices and cordials

### Aspall
*Organic apple and pear juices*
The Cyder House, Aspall Hall,
Stowmarket, Suffolk IP14 6PD
www.aspall.co.uk
info@aspall.co.uk
Tel: 01728 860510
Fax: 01728 861031

### Belvoir Fruit Cordials
*Blackcurrant, lemon, ginger and
elderflower cordials*
Belvoir, Grantham, Lincs NG32 1PB
Tel: 01476 870286
Fax: 01476 870114

### David Berryman Ltd
*Bulk fruit juice concentrates*
Unit 10 Park Industrial Estate,
Frogmore, St Albans, Herts AL2 2DR
Tel: 01727 874478
Fax: 01727 874476

### Ella Drinks Ltd
*Raspberry juice*
Alloa Business Centre, Alloa,
Clackmannanshire FK10 3SA
info@bouvrage.com
Tel: 01259 721905
Fax: 01786 834074

### The Organic Food Company
*Carrot, vegetable and beetroot juices*
Unit 2 Blacknest Industrial Estate,
Blacknest Rd, Alton, Hants GU34 4PX
sarah@tofco.free-online.co.uk
Tel: 01420 520530
Fax: 01420 23985

### Rocks Organic Cordials
*Wide range of organic friuit cordials*
Loddon Park Farm, New Bath Road,
Twyford, Berks RG10 9RY
Tel: 0118 934 2344
Fax: 0118 934 4539

## Herbs

### Hambleden Herbs
*Full range of medicinal and culinary
herbs, and organic herb teas*
Court Farm, Milverton, Taunton,
Somerset TA4 1NF
www.hambledenherbs.co.uk
info@hambledenherbs.co.uk
Tel: 01823 401205
Fax: 01823 400276

### Herbal Apothecary
*Full range of medicinal herbs*
103 High Street, Syston,
Leics LE7 1GQ
www.herbalapothecary.net
Tel: 0116 260 2690
Fax: 0116 2600 2757

### Neals Yard Remedies
*Mail order herbs; full Neals
Yard range*
29 John Dalton Street,
Manchester M2 6DS
mail@nealsyardremedies.com
Tel: 0161 831 7875
Fax: 0161 835 9322

### Phyto Pharmaceuticals
*Fresh plant, herb and vegetable
juices and medicinal herbs*
Park Works, Park Road, Mansfield,
Woodhouse, Notts NG19 8EF
Tel: 01623 644334
Fax: 01623 657232

## Health drinks

### Bottle Green Drinks Company
*Wide range of cordials including
elderflower, ginger and lemongrass*
Frogmarsh Mills, South Woodchester,
Stroud, Glos GL5 5ET
www.bottlegreen.co.uk
info@bottlegreen.co.uk
Tel: 01453 872882
Fax: 01453 872188

### Cranley Fresh Foods
*Organic drinks*
80-100 Gwynne Rd, London SW11 3UW
Tel: 020 7223 8283
Fax: 020 7585 3830

### Kombucha Health Ltd
*Kombucha*
Unit A3B, New Brunswick Business
Centre, Liverpool L3 4BD
www.merseyworld.com/kombucha
Tel: 0151 709 0008
Fax: 0151 733 9463

### Pete & Johnny Plc
*Smoothies*
15 Lots Road, Chelsea Wharf,
London SW10 0OJ
www.p-j.co.uk
info@p-j.co.uk
Tel: 020 7352 1276
Fax: 020 7376 7101

### Provamel
*Soya-based non-dairy products
including milk, cream and yogurt*
Ashley House, 86-94 High Street,
Hounslow, Middx TW3 1NH
www.provamel.co.uk
provamel@vdmuk-rs.co.uk
Tel: 020 8577 2727
Fax: 020 8570 9364

### Resurrection Drinks Ltd
*Functional tonics and syrups*
4 Evans Road, Bristol BS6 6TQ
www.resurrection.co.uk
info@resurrection.co.uk
Tel/fax: 0117 907 9631

**Ridgeway's Fair Trade Teas**
*Organic teas*
PO Box 8, Pasture Road, Moreton,
Wirral, Merseyside L46 8XF
Tel: 0151 522 4975
Fax: 0151 522 4921

**R. Twining and Co. Ltd**
*Organic teas and herb teas*
South Way, Andover, Hants SP10 5AQ
Tel: 01264 334477
Fax: 01264 337177

**Windmill Organics**
*Organic cranberry drink; distributor
for many organic brands*
66 Meadow Close, London SW20 9JD
Tel: 020 8395 9749
Fax: 020 8286 4732

## Fresh produce

**Soil Association**
*Up-to-date listing of locations
and times for farmers' markets,
where farmers sell produce direct
to the public*
Bristol House, 40-56 Victoria Street,
Bristol BS1 6BY
domlane@soilassociation.org
Tel: 0117 914 2451
Fax: 0117 925 2504

**Langridge Organic Products Ltd**
*Grower and supplier of organic
produce*
Unit A55-A57, New Covent Garden,
London SW8 5NX
Tel: 020 7622 7440
Fax: 020 7622 7441

**Jayes & Company Ltd**
*Organic fruit and vegetables from
around the world*
5 Badgebury Rise, Marlow Bottom,
Marlow, Bucks SL7 3QA
Jayes@dial.pipex.com
Tel: 01628 483422
Fax: 01628 483560

## Equipment
**Kitchens (Catering Utensils) Ltd**
*Wide range of juicers, blenders and
other appliances; will do mail order*
167 Whiteladies Road,
Bristol BS8 2SQ
Tel: 0117 973 9614
Fax: 0117 923 8565

**Robot Coupe (UK) Ltd**
*Waring juicers, blenders and mixers*
Unit 2, Fleming Way, Worton Road
Industrial Estate, Isleworth,
Middx TW7 6EU
sales@robotcoupe.demon.co.uk
Tel: 020 8232 8171

**Wholistic Research Company Ltd**
*Juicers, water distillers, books*
The Old Forge, Mill Green,
Hatfield AL9 5NZ
www.WholisticResearch.com
Tel: 01707 262686
Fax: 01707 258828

**International Health Products Ltd**
*Commercial juice extractors*
54B Minerva Road, Park Royal,
London NW10 6HJ
IHPuk@city2000.Net
Tel: 020 8961 7711
Fax: 07070 606310

**La Cuisinière**
*Wide range of juicers, blenders and
other appliances; catalogue available,
will do mail order*
81-83 Northcote Road,
London SW11 6PJ
Tel/fax: 020 7223 4487

# recipe index

page numbers underlined indicate
recipes which are illustrated

# general index

for recipes, see recipe index on pages 154-5

page numbers in **bold** indicate key ingredients described in chapter one

### a

cooling properties 137
flu 78
immune system 64
cumin 88
cystitis 122-3

**d**

dandelion 50, 132
dates 59, 135
Daucarine 19
decongestants 21, 23, 27, 36-8, 87
depression 25, 128, 146-7
diabetes 25, 28, 30, 31, 34
diarrhoea 108-9, 112
digestive system 47
dill 49, 90, 106, 107
diverticulitis 110-11
dried foods 15, 149
drug withdrawal 25
dysentery 30, 34, 37

**e**

*E. coli* 20, 30, 32, 43, 109
earache 35
eczema 19, 22, 32
elderberry 140
elderflower 78, 85, 136
emotional healing 142-3
energy boosters 56-9, 132-3
equipment 148, 153
exercise 48
expectorants 19, 21, 37, 41-2, 74-5
eyes 19, 52-3

**f**

feeling good, drinks for 45-69
feet, cold 96-7
fennel 50, 106, 113
fertility 31, 42
fevers, children's 86-7
fibre 100, 112
finishing touches 149
flatulence 104-5, 112
flu 78-9, 84-5
*see also* colds
fluid retention 48-9, 124-5
food processors 148
frozen foods 149
fruit 14, 15, 149
*see also* individual fruits

**g**

gall-stones 21
garlic **34**, 132, 144
blood pressure 98, 99
candidiasis 119
circulation 97
colic 107
energy booster 59
immune system 62, 63, 64
gastritis 22-5, 27-8, 33
gastroenteritis 23
ginger **37**, 132, 144
brain booster 66
calming effects 135
candidiasis 118
coughs 74
energy booster 56, 57, 58
flu 79
IBS 113
immune system 63
nausea 116, 117
sore throats 76
ginseng **31**, 65, 68
glucose 66
gout 19-20, 28, 32, 39, 40-2
grape 100, 114, 125
grapefruit
anaemia 95
circulation 96
flatulence 105
haemorrhoids 114
hangovers 88
immune system 64
sinusitis 84
weight loss 48
gripe water 106
guava 84

**h**

haemorrhoids 114-15
hair 60-1
hands, cold 96-7
hangovers 88-9
hawthorn 99
hay fever 22, 23, 34
headaches 82-3
heart disease 19, 24, 26, 34-6, 40
heartburn 102-3
heartsease 143

herbal teas 13
for feeling good 63, 65-7
for illness 78-9, 86, 91, 99, 103, 105-7, 109, 113, 116, 120-1
for looking good 50, 54
preparation 149
for the spirit 141, 146-7
herbs 18, 152
*see also* individual herbs
herpes simplex 22, 28
hiccoughs 21
honey
anaemia 95
arthritis 92
catarrhal congestion 81
diarrhoea 108, 109
flatulence 104
IBS 112
warming properties 141
hormones 120

**i**

IBS *see* irritable bowel syndrome
illness, drinks for recovery 71-125
immune system
boosters 62-5
requirements 46
impotence 42
infertility 36
ingredients
choosing 15, 149
key 17-43
insomnia 90-1
intestinal flora
candidiasis 118
constipation 100
dietary boosters 24, 34, 41, 43
flatulence 104
intestinal parasites 19, 21, 36, 38, 42
irritable bowel syndrome (IBS) 112-13

**j**

juice fasting 149
juicers 148
juices 14
for feeling good 64
for illness 75, 83-4, 93, 100, 105, 114, 123-5
for looking good 52
sources 152
for the spirit 140

## acknowledgments

The publishers would like to thank the following for their help in the production of this book: Bridget Morley, Jo Godfrey Wood, Beverly LeBlanc, Caroline Sutton, Lisa Footitt, Lynn Bresler, Matt Moate, Harriet Epstein and Darry McKay. Also, Anne at La Cuisinière (for supplying stainless steel kitchenware for photography)

## The Complete Womans Herbal

**Anne McIntyre**  ISBN 1 85675 135 X  £15.99
*A practical guide to using herbs for healing through every cycle of a woman's life from adolescence to menopause.*

## The Complete Floral Healer

**Anne McIntyre**  ISBN 1 85675 067 1  £15.99
*Comprehensive guide to the flowers used in aromatherapy, herbal remedies and flower essences.*

## Herbs for Common Ailments

**Anne McIntyre**  ISBN 1 85675 055 8  £8.99
*Select and use herbs for effective, natural treatments.*

## Simple Home Remedies for Common Ailments

**Anne McIntyre**  ISBN 1 85675 086 8  £8.99
*Natural cures from your kitchen, bathroom and garden.*

## The Detox Plan

**Jane Alexander**  ISBN 1 85675 156 2  £10.99
*Weekend detox programmes for peak performance.*

## Energy Drinks

**Friedrich Bohlmann**  ISBN 1 85675 140 6  £4.99
*Fresh juices packed full of goodness for vitality and health.*

To order a book or request a catalogue contact:
Gaia Books Ltd, 20 High Street, Stroud, Glos GL5 1AZ
T: 01453 752985  F: 01453 752987  E: info@gaiabooks.co.uk

visit our web site to see a complete list of our titles: www.gaiabooks.co.uk